Time To Be

Acknowledge &

Live

In (your)

Vibrational

Essence

By:
Mary Electra
www.maryelectra.com

Edited by Eileen Bray
contact Eileen at **eileens_uk@yahoo.com**

Cover Art by Michael Gaeta
Contact Michael at **runicnomad@gmail.com**

Author contact:
www.maryelectra.com
ISBN: 978-0-578-03104-0

Ancient Sounds Publishing

Acknowledgments

This book is dedicated to all the people who have encouraged me, stood by me, supported me, and accepted my craziness. There have been good times and rough times, but through it all those people near and dear to me have been there. Without you this book would have never been a reality. A special thanks to Sandra Assasnik and Eileen Bray for their help in formatting and editing my book. Last, but not least, I also dedicate this to each and every person who reads it, for you are the future.

Table of Contents

Introduction

Introduction

Hello,

After years of resistance, I've finally written a book.

What can I share with you about this book?

I don't think I've ever received an astrology reading since I've been an adult where I have not been asked if I was writing a book, or told I needed to write a book. The answer was always: "No, I write poetry and I write songs, but I don't write books. Anyway there are plenty of books, and what do I have to say that hasn't already been said?"

In the meantime to appease the spirits I wrote a poetry book and a recipe book, and thought to myself, "there I've written a book, not just one but two, so this should make the spirits happy!"

So, what is this? Another book!

This book began after I had come through a seven year period of my most challenging earth experiences. I sat down to record my thoughts, and process this monumental experience, as writing is the method I use to process my feelings. In the past this process has usually been through poetry or letters to Me/God, always something short and sweet. So you can imagine my surprise of what transpired!

Once I began to write, it was almost like it took me over. Every morning and every night I was writing frantically. It was as if I didn't write fast enough the information would evaporate and be lost. I had to record what was pulsing through me. It soon became evident this was going to be more than just a few thoughts; this was turning into a book. I sensed that whatever I was writing was going to be the start of something new or different for me, so I was curious about that. That curiosity has kept me going throughout this entire process. The first draft took less than a month, and you don't want to ask how long or laborious the editing process is; but now I have a book. This is part autobiographical, sharing a brief overview of my life and how I was led to write this book, my insights relating to energy, sound and our higher consciousness and my understanding of our pressing need to acknowledge and know our power as a "spark" of the divine light.

I do hope this finally makes the spirits happy, and that in some small way those who read it will find themselves somewhere within the pages, and be inspired to be "ALIVE" (Acknowledge & Live In "your" Vibrational Essence).

We are in precarious times, and it is time to awaken to what is happening around us, and to the power that exists within us. This book encourages you and challenges you to live in your "Cosmic Consciousness". There are probing questions and interesting stories.

So, what do I have to say that hasn't already been said? In truth nothing really, and yet sometimes things just need to be said a thousand times in a thousand different ways before they can be heard and/or understood.

Introduction

Since you're reading this, I guess I can safely assume that you have chosen to read my book, and I would like to take this time to thank you for honoring my words with your time. Blessings be to you.

Mary Electra
2009

Time to Be ALIVE

Book One

Part I
My Beginning

Chapter 1

As long as I can remember I knew and still know there is a purpose for me being here. I fought to be here (which is a story for another book) and once I arrived there has always been this underlying awareness that I came here for a reason. I was part of something greater, something that tugged at me and seemed to always be there under the surface, and for many years remained unclear to me. It took some time for me to grow into my clarity as you will see.

From the time I was 2 or 3 years old I had dreams about a sense of my purpose. I also had visitors of the creepy crawly variety in my crib with me at night time. There were snakes, lizards and frogs. They were always there in a surreal way. They were only there at night and in hindsight I realize these creatures were probably guiding and protecting me but at the time I didn't understand that. The visitors and the dreams were frightening and very unsettling for me as a child. The visitors left when I was around 6 but the dreams lived with me into my young adulthood.

As a young child I had other personal torments that I was living through and I found myself developing into a very serious and contemplative child; in fact I don't really have many memories of being carefree at all, so these dreams and my visitors were just another issue I had to contend with.

Author's Note: *Now, of course, I understand some of the messages the dreams were giving me, but at the time I just had to live with them. As I became a young adult, this connection to something greater continued to haunt me, but it was on a very subliminal level, and I was not as conscious then as I am now. Until the age of two, children have amazing awareness, which subsides with age. I believe this has to do with the fact that newborns have an active thymus until they are two at which time it shrinks. I feel an active thymus provides babies with the ability to move and communicate freely between dimensions, and this ability ceases as the thymus shrinks.*

As I grew older, I somehow connected the dreams and my visitors with my awareness of being here for a purpose. It was all part of some bigger picture, and I don't really know how but intuitively I was able to grasp this, and in reflection I knew, consciously or unconsciously, there were always angels near me and they were protecting me.

Somehow I managed to survive my youth somewhat intact and was continuing on with my life. But as I said before, there was always something prodding me. After all, there was a reason for my being here and I knew this in a deep and "knowing" way; but not necessarily in a conscious way. So just to be sure that I had a conscious awareness of it, the greater powers made sure I had several confirmations of this as I grew older leaving no room in my sometimes nimble and often confused mind for any doubt.

Book One
Part I

Author's Note: *Remember my statement about angels? I feel these reminders were apart of the bigger scheme, and the angels or messages always seem to be there when I most needed them.*

My first memory of receiving one of these confirming reminders was when I was 17 and I met a very gifted palm reader who read my palms. The information I received from him was uncanny. How he knew what he knew was baffling. I am pretty certain the information he imparted would qualify this as a psychic reading. This was my first experience delving into the realm of the intuitive world through someone else's eyes.

Not only was the information baffling, but how he came to me was mysterious. My sister, my nephew, one of my school friends and I lived together in Seaside, next to Fort Ord. It was during the time of the Vietnam War so a lot of boys were being cycled through there preparing for the war. My roommate's boyfriend was in the military. One day this very handsome man, driving a sports car, drove by the apartments and asked me if my roommate's boyfriend was there. He told me he was a friend of his and was suppose to meet him. No one else was home so I invited him in to wait, and we struck up a conversation that led to the subject of palmistry. This conversation then turned into a demonstration, which led to a full blown reading. I was in awe of his ability. He knew everything about my childhood. Things I had not told anyone, he knew. With ease he transition into reading my future. He confirmed I had chosen to come to this planet for a reason, and I would not be engaged in the full expression of my purpose until I reached my mid–forties. He was encouraging me to fulfill my purpose and not get lost in the illusion of this world. Some of what he told me confounded me, other things excited me, but what he knew and how he knew it intrigued me. We spent the whole afternoon talking, and as I reflect on it now, connecting.

What I thought to be most interesting was my roommate and her boyfriend never showed up that afternoon. Another interesting fact was when I reported to my roommate's boyfriend that one of his friends had stopped by, he was puzzled. He had never heard of this person, and had not asked anyone to meet him at our apartment.

This person was a mystery. It was as if he magically appeared and just as magically disappeared, and for some time his presence remained a mystery to me.

Author's Note: *At the time he entered my life I had never heard of an avatar, but after I read about avatars in Linda Goodman's "Star Signs", my immediate thought turned to this mysterious man I had encountered when I was seventeen.*

For those of you who have not heard of an avatar, I will give you the dictionary's definition:

Ava-tar; 1. Hinduism **a god appearing on earth in bodily form; incarnation of a god** 2. any incarnation or embodiment, as a quality or concept of a person.

Once I heard and understood what an avatar was, I had no doubt that I had been visited by just such a being. Who else could appear out of nowhere and have so much accurate information concerning my past, present and future? An avatar makes sense to me. Whoever and whatever he was, his presence in my life had a profound effect on me.

So that was my first unexpected confirmation of my childhood "knowing", but I was soon to have another. When I was twenty I attended a Halloween party, and part of the party's entertainment was a psychic that had been paid to do brief readings for each of the guests. When she gave me my reading, she told me I was a very gifted being with great wisdom, and I had come to this planet for a reason. I had a purpose and I would not engage in this purpose until I turned forty–five, and at that point, I would know my greatest joy in my later years. She told me that in my younger years I had things to "work" out on this planet and would have challenging times, but she would not embellish on this, and just kept reiterating to me that I was not to lose my faith.

These two people had confirmed an awareness I had since I was a pre-school child. After those two encounters I could not help but wonder about the messages. What was this purpose, and why me? I was curious, but since this wasn't going to happen until I was in my forties, I still had a few years to see how it would all play out, so all I could do was go on about my life.

By the time I received these readings, the dreams I mentioned earlier that had began as a child had become more vivid and I knew, as I mentioned earlier, they had something to do with my reason for being here. The dreams continued to be a bit unsettling for me. Since they started when I was two or three years old, I didn't have the tools to interpret then until I became older, and even then, I was not exactly sure what the dreams were saying. I can share with you now that for the longest time, because of these dreams, I dreaded what was in store for me. It frightened me, and there was a part of me that just didn't want to be around for the experience. It all felt so overwhelming. If I'm being honest as I am writing this, I realize there are brief moments today when it still does frighten me.

Along with this deeper sense of having a purpose I also had an affinity with the esoteric world, even before I understood there was an esoteric world.

There are several examples of this from my childhood that stand out which I will share at this time. My mother used to delight in relating this story to people about when we would visit her best friend, who had a strong interest in astrology. When we went to visit her friend, I would immediately head for her magazine rack and pull out her astrology magazines and sit and page through these magazines. I would do this during the whole visit! I was perhaps three or four and could not read. These magazines were filled with text; copies of charts and glyphs, nothing I could *supposedly* understand. They did not contain bright colors or pictures to stimulate me, but apparently I poured over these magazines for hours, much to the fascination of my mother and her friend.

To this day I believe somewhere in my knowing self I recognized and understood these glyphs and charts. They were familiar to me and that is why they always captured my attention.

Author's Note: *I strongly feel this is a clear example of having cognitive recognition of something familiar from our deep internal knowingness. I also feel we have these*

Book One
Part I

flashes of cognitive recognition often as children. We just do not know how to assimilate or utilize them.

Another interesting tale of my youth was something I use to do when I was around six or seven years of age. I would tell the other neighborhood children that I was adopted. Of course everyone knew this was not true, and they would challenge me and attempt to convince me otherwise. I clearly remember my retort being: "I know I was born to my mother, but I'm really adopted, I'm really a star."

Author's Note: *Was I talking about being a "star", or was I remembering being from a star system? What did I know at that early age?*

There is another memory of my quirkiness from my childhood that I feel is relevant to this story. I was born in the Midwest, and I cannot ever remember feeling at home where I lived. I could never truly breathe where I was born. When I was five, I had a bicycle, I would take my bicycle to the railroad tracks two blocks from where I lived and I would follow the tracks thinking, "If I can just follow these tracks they will take me home. I didn't even know what direction I was going, but I just knew if I followed them they would take me home." Of course when it started getting dark, I would become afraid and turn my bicycle around and head back to the house where I lived. For several years I continued to go to those tracks in hopes of finding my way home. At some point, I realized this was a useless exercise, and I gave up my little treks following the railroad tracks, but I did not give up on my desire to find "my" home.

Time to Be ALIVE

I remember, as if it were yesterday, the first time I felt like I was home, the first time I felt that I could breathe. We were on a vacation. I was thirteen years old and I was standing on a beach in California looking out over the Pacific Ocean. It felt so good to finally breathe. I was finally home. It would take several years more before I could call California my home, but I did eventually return to live there. I distinctly remember feeling now I could finally begin to live my life. This was my beginning of a new dawn.

Author's Note: *Oddly enough when I came to California, which is where I call home, to live for good, I took a train. What did I know?*

As I got older my interest moved from an unconscious interest to a conscious interest in the esoteric world. In looking back to my childhood, I realized I always felt estranged from others, and in part my esoteric interest was one of the reasons why. It was not the only reason nor was it a major reason that I felt separate from others. As a young child and pre-teen I had several issues in my life that contributed to my feelings of alienation, and that certainly played a part in my troubled youth. In fairness, my interest in the esoteric world, conscious or unconscious, was eventually my saving grace, and it is only with the reflection of writing this that I can see that. Even then, I had a foot in two worlds.

As I mentioned before, most of my youth I felt separate, and different than everyone else. When I was a teenager and young adult, I had the strongest desires to be a normal person (whatever normal is), but I could not shake my childhood realities or my esoteric interest, for they were a part of me.

Book One
Part I

Author's Note: *It is so interesting to reflect on how important the approval of our peers is in our youth. This inward struggle was emotionally difficult for me, and if the truth be told that struggle still bears its scars today, every now and again, but age and maturity has had a way of settling the discomfort even if it has not been erased.*

This brought about difficulties for me: the internal struggle of desperately wanting to be part of the circle; and, on the flip side feeling I was always on the outside of the circle. However difficult it seemed at the time, life does have a way of going on, and I found myself growing into a young woman, and with me came the struggle. The older I became, the more difficult it was to dispel my unusual interest. But, the time had come for me to go to work and I was faced with the dilemma of going into the real world. I felt ill-prepared for my leap into the grown up world, and my choices were limited. I was going to have to work.

When I was seventeen it felt like I had very few choices in my life. Because of my tormented childhood I left home at the age of sixteen to live with my sister and her child. As grateful as I was for my sister's graciousness, I knew I could not live with my sister and her child forever. While I was living with her I was becoming my nephew's nanny while my sister was out having fun. I knew I had to get a job and find a place of my own if I was ever really going to grow up. In my mind I had very few skills, and the option of marriage didn't seem like a viable alternative and entering the military was out of the question. My interest was in astrology, numerology, palmistry (because of my avatar experience), and tarot. How would these interests prepare me for a life in the working world? How was I going to reconcile my interest in the esoteric with filing, typing and bookkeeping? How was I ever going to make it as an adult? I must admit I was scared and troubled, and did not feel like I had a lot of options so I attempted suicide. It was a lame attempt and as I was laying there sick from all the pills I'd taken, I began to wonder what my life would become. I was very curious and I needed to see what life had in store for me. I knew I needed to stick around to see what was going to happen, so I made myself throw up.

Author's Note: *There is always something positive in every experience, even when it seems to be hidden from us. Prior to my "suicide" attempt, I felt I was forced to be here, even though initially I had fought to be here. My life's circumstances were difficult, and there were so many times I didn't want to live or be a part of this. I didn't feel that I had a choice, and I was resentful because of that. That thought process took me directly into victim consciousness, but somehow laying there that night, and feeling curious, I consciously made a choice to go on. I consciously became responsible for my life, and as difficult as it is sometimes, I recognize I am responsible for everything that happens in my world. Good, bad or indifferent. As I write this, I also realize there are still times I try to run from that responsibility. I attempt to look outside myself, but in the end I consciously know that I am creating my world. So even though I can wear the mask of victim quite well, at the end of the day, I know, I create my reality. And, as you read earlier, I have angels that are here to assist me and guide me.*

Book One
Part I

Chapter 2

So after all was said and done, after acting out my fear, I ventured into this expansive world! I still wasn't clear how my esoteric interest would play out in my "ordinary" day–to–day life. I was so busy facing the reality of figuring out how I was going to fit into the world from a survival point of view that I didn't have much time to think about much more. As I stated before I was ill prepared for this world, and my skills were limited so I didn't have a clue what I was going to do, let alone how to integrate my deeper interest into my everyday life.

From the very beginning I was having a difficult time with my work situation. Soon after my lame suicide attempt, I left my sister and I started working. I was seventeen going on eighteen and the being that I was just could not coexist with the structures of a 9–to–5 job. For years I struggled with this. I had more jobs than a centipede has legs. My employment record for the first two or three years of my working life looked more like a train schedule than a work record. I just could not go to a job that bored me for eight hours no matter how badly I needed the money. So I aimlessly drifted from one job to another. I must admit I had a lot of useful work experiences, but nothing captured my heart. When I came into my early twenties, I stumbled onto a career that suited me perfectly. I obtained a position as a clerk in the credit department of a large corporation. Certain circumstances transpired, and within six months, I was in charge of the department. Not with a title but with the responsibilities. It seemed as if this position was tailor made for my skills. Once I was given the responsibility of the department, I set up a system and turned their receivables around in about six months time. I continued to maintain a very impressive collection record until the day I left. My abilities were making this company a lot of money and I felt like I deserved to be acknowledged for this. I asked to be promoted to Credit Manager and have the title as well as the compensation for the job I was already doing. As I was not yet twenty–three years old and I had the distinction of being a female, I was told it would not be possible to promote me. Needless to say, I left. Don't ask me where I got the courage. I just couldn't stay under those circumstances.

After leaving this position, I wandered from place to place for another three years or so until it became painfully clear that I needed to have my own business to make the money I deserved, do the kind of work that suited my talents and have the work schedule I desired. Shortly before the age of twenty–seven, out of the ethers, I created a career for myself as a "business consultant" in cash management. This new career would allow me time as well as the financial resources I needed to explore my other interest. Time was an important commodity for me. I needed time so I could concentrate on coming to terms with my spiritual interest as well as integrate them into the physical world.

Author's Note: *I find it interesting that when I came into the real world, I started to understand myself without trying. I manifested jobs and opportunities without conscious awareness. Somehow my inner abilities were shining through, and I was actually living in my "cosmic" consciousness. I was allowing the process to happen. It is amazing for me to be writing this and reflecting on my life, and be able to see the magic that I can be.*

Book One
Part I

Roughly at the same time I created this profession for myself, by the grace of God/Goddess, I began drawing other like–minded people into my life. I was soon surrounded with people and friends that had an esoteric interest as well as psychic abilities. I remember being awed by their psychic abilities; yet deep inside of me I had this sense of knowing, and along with this sense of knowing an understanding that within me lived many abilities, but to fully realize them I needed to remember them. I told one of my good friends this morsel of intuition, and she just smiled in this mysterious but *knowing* way. She somehow knew I was soon to be awakened.

During this same period of time I had another dear friend who had many psychic abilities and one of those abilities was seeing peoples' auras. I marveled at this and desired to see auras as well. She was so wonderful and gracious. She worked with me a whole evening until I also could see auras. The esoteric world had captured me completely.

For a short time after that experience I continued to walk between two worlds thinking that if I crossed over to my spiritual path I could never go back to the familiar world that I had become accustomed to. For some insane reason, I felt I had to make a decision and this was a struggle for me.

Author's Note: *As I reflect on this now, I know there was a part of me that felt like it was interesting to even be having that struggle between my mundane reality and my esoteric reality. When it came to my day–to–day existence in the mundane world, I think from an observational point of view, it would be fair for me to say the mundane was only familiar to me because it existed around me, not in me. I just did not feel compatible with what I observed as the way of life people seemed to engage in. From my observation, people seemed to work everyday in jobs that do not fulfill them; they complain about their job but never change them. People seem to struggle with their natural feelings and with their feelings towards others. The games between men and women were the most baffling of all. This "game," as I call it, has always been interesting to me, and to this day is still something I have trouble understanding. There always seemed to be some kind of rule book or book of survival that I wasn't privy to, and because of this I was experiencing a great deal of angst. I also could not close my eyes to my deeper needs, i.e. my need to be happy in the work I did, the freedom to express my feelings without being guarded, to love without being afraid. So why was I having the struggle in the first place? Even though I had this undeniable discomfort with the world I perceived to be "normal"; I was still attempting to be "normal". Go figure. Please believe me when I tell you, to this day, I still do not know what "normal" really is, yet to be in truth I know back then that was a major part of my consideration. Even though I still have not figured out what normal is, I understand in our attempt to be normal, we lose our understanding of "natural". Natural is where our instincts live. Even though it took some time for me to realize it, my desire now is to view the world through my "natural" eyes.*

Even though I was fascinated with the esoteric world and my exploration of this world felt familiar and ever so appealing, it appeared to me that the masses, for the most part lived within the walls of the mundane world. Did I have the courage to leave this "safe" world and follow the spiritual path? Could I let go of this desire to be "normal"? In the end as I'm sure you have surmised, my spiritual path won out. I just could not deny myself, nor could I deny this deep intrinsic knowing any longer.

Time to Be ALIVE

Book One
Part I

Chapter 3

After turning thirty, while I was still a "business consultant," I finally crossed the threshold into the spiritual world with total conviction. I delved into my studies with vigor. Since I had already created a reality that gave me the time I needed, I was free to explore to my heart's desire. I was free to prepare myself for what was coming. I began studying more seriously the things that had always captured my attention, such as tarot, astrology, numerology and the I Ch'ing. I was on my path, but I felt like I still had to figure out how to bring the spiritual aspects of myself into the "mundane" world where I still spent many hours.

Author's Note: *I strongly feel our creative center is important to our spiritual endeavors, so mixed in with my esoteric studies I also explored my creative self.*

Since I could never really hide my interest in the esoteric world, I needed to accept it and go from there. Good, bad or indifferent this is who I was, and it always seemed to seep out of me. Even when I made attempts to hide it, it would creep out. When I was working as a consultant in the banking world I would talk about astrology and energy like I would talk about my assessment of the percentage of collectable receivables. I just could not help myself!

I admit I was looked upon as "strange" because we so evidently live in a world where almost everyone seeks to be "normal." I felt that people were curious even though they would not outright admit to it. I feel, for the most part, they secretly considered it interesting. So even though the two worlds seemed like water and oil, in my experience when I came from a place of truth and sincerity there always seemed to be tolerance, mixed with some amusement and if I'm not mistaken, a certain amount of curiosity.

So I guess in answer to my own question, "How do I mix the two worlds"? My answer would be *naturally*.

Author's Note: *Writing this offers me the opportunity to reflect. In that reflection I feel that my initial worry was greater than the reality warranted, as is the case in many new adventures. I also have the opportunity to observe how much I waiver. So I encourage you, as well as myself, to move beyond the worry; for you never know, a miracle might be waiting right around the corner.*

At around thirty–one years of age, again during my time as a "business consultant," I began to study color and season and its relationship with make-up artistry. As a woman who rarely wears make-up this was indeed an interesting turn of events. I remember feeling that if we could remove people's masks and enhance their true beauty it would make the world a better place to live, and perhaps even begin to support the rebalance of earth.

Author's Note: *I realize this might seem to be a stretch to consider make-up somehow supporting the balance of earth, but my instincts looked at it differently, and I have this habit, as I am observing through this writing, of eventually following my instincts. I need to share with you that this reflection is as interesting to me as I hope it is to you: for I am seeing myself through different eyes, and I'm quite amused and amazed at what I am seeing.*

Book One
Part I

For some reason, this line of work felt more congruent with whom I understood myself to be. I did not have a clear intellectual awareness of why I felt this way, I just did and I went with my instinctual sense and for about six years I apprenticed with a woman in this field. I learned a lot about myself during this time. I found that I loved working with women, and I realized I was using a rather esoteric approach to discover their complementary colors as well as their inner beauty and "vibrational" essence. Unbeknownst to me at the time this world of make-up, color and seasonal energy was leading me towards another path.

Time to Be ALIVE

Chapter 4

This was my beginning in consciously understanding the vibration of beings. Simply speaking color and human beings are vibration. When you use the colors that vibrate best with your inner-self then you can present yourself to the world in a more authentic way. This is a simple yet effective way to express who you are by using compatible colors to assist you in presenting your vibrational harmony.

With this background, I began to understand the world as energy and vibration, which plays a major role in the gifts I am here to share with the world. Even though this career was not my path as I later found out, it was a stepping stone to other things that lay ahead for me.

Time to Be ALIVE

Book One
Part I

Chapter 5

I was finishing with my career in the financial world when I started seriously exploring the creative aspects of myself. My consulting career was waning so to speak, and was no longer harmonious with my ever–expanding spirit. I needed to find another avenue to satisfy my financial needs.

At this same time I also became involved in a relationship, which offered another twist to my spiritual development.

Author's Note: *Relationships are good for spiritual development as they stretch you in ways you cannot stretch yourself. They are constant mirrors and I believe they allow us to see ourselves through different eyes.*

It was during this time I shifted my career focus from the financial world to sales. There was as an added bonus to this career as it offered me the opportunity to learn a great deal about marketing and ad designs. This, of course, played into my desire to explore my creative expression, not to mention the opportunity to work with people and assist them in their business endeavors. I was turning my skills and abilities into a service for others. As time went, on I began to realize that being of service to people is one of the major motivating factors in the career choices I make, and service is a key element in the spiritual work I am on the planet to do.

It was interesting to me how my life was unfolding. When I was seventeen I hadn't even had the imagination to imagine any of the experiences I would be having, I had only been curious enough to live to experience it. As you are well aware, at that age I was afraid and nervous and feeling very ill–prepared for entering into the world of adulthood. I have realized that if we can just allow ourselves to step into the experiences life has to offer us we might be pleasantly surprised at what's in store for us. Having said this, I still often go kicking and screaming into new adventures.

Chapter 6

Let's review for a moment. As earlier mentioned, I realize I was not cut out for working in a 9-to-5 environment. To survive I had to manifest a career that utilized my skills which, at the time, seemed limited. I did not have a college education, and the job opportunities available to me were clerical in nature and this was just not my forte. My skills consisted of talking—and let me think now—talking. Armed with this knowledge and the desire to have more flexibility in my life I manifested first my career in cash management, and then sales. Both were careers that provided me with the financial resources I needed, the flexibility to explore myself, and best of all I had used my own pool or resources to create them. Would this be "Manifesting 101"?

Thus far I had figured out a way to survive in a way that was tolerable for me, explored myself and my creative abilities, and manifest my creative abilities into reality. I had come a long way from that confused and afraid yet curious and soulful child of so many years ago.

I was coming closer and closer to my 45th birthday. Even though I had created a way to make money and still have the flexibility to explore my esoteric interest, I still did not have a clue as to what I was going to do or be. I just kept putting one foot in front of the other and assumed it would be revealed to me, while I kept on exploring as well as healing. My study of tarot became fairly refined, so much so that my friends were always asking me to give readings for them. I also studied dreams and became a member of a dream group for several years. I played at making pottery which I thought was great fun, especially working with the colors of the glazes. Pottery is very humbling, and you soon realize the clay is in charge. I was expanding, and exploring, and somehow, don't ask me how, I was just being and allowing the process to unfold.

I also love to touch, and people like to be touched by me. In my younger years I used that ability as a form of seduction, and I might add it served me well. I had a lover for many years, and he always told me I had the best hands. He said this so much I started thinking that I might take a massage course as part of my explorations into my deeper spiritual self. Little did I know how important that little "seed" of inspiration would become!

Chapter 7

I actually began my career in massage as a fluke. I was selling advertising and on the side I did tarot readings. One day I just happened to be giving a tarot reading to a client the day after I had seen my lover. Several days before a friend who had just finished massage school had let me borrow her massage table so I could give my lover a massage on a real massage table. Now remember this is the lover who kept encouraging me to do massage, so in the back of my mind the seed had already been planted. When my tarot client saw the massage table sitting in my living room she asked me if I did massage, and without any hesitation or thought I just said, "YES". Her regular therapist was out of town and her neck was bothering her so she asked me how much it would cost her to do a massage. Without any consideration I told her it was the same price as her reading, so she decided to have a massage as well as a reading. After the massage she told me I was better than her regular massage therapist. The minute she left I called a massage school to find out about taking classes. This was on a Thursday and the following Tuesday I was studying massage. I was forty-four years old.

What a turn of events. The last thing in the world I had ever imagined doing was becoming a massage therapist.

Author's Note: *Funny how things pop into our lives in what seems to be a random way. Could there really be a bigger picture?*

Time to Be ALIVE

I remember when I decided to study massage, my friends were not what I would consider supportive of my choice. When I started school I had a very lucrative career selling advertising, and there were hundreds if not thousands of people who were certified massage therapists and at the same time starving. I would not be daunted, this was one of those occasions that my instincts were strong and I could not and would not deny them. Within two months of graduation I was working for two chiropractors.

It was clear from the start there was truly magic in my hands and I remembered thinking "so this is how I will touch thousands of people". I marveled at the wonder of it all. When I worked on people they would often see images of Mother Mary, The Christ Consciousness, Sai Baba, and other energy forces. This was the start of a new adventure, for a whole new reality was opening to me. Finally my spiritual world and my physical world became one. When I was doing my "work," time stood still, and I was in bliss. Magic was happening in my life, and the most amazing thing I'd like to share with all of you was this was just the beginning. There were many more doorways waiting to be opened to me. Most importantly I was available and willing to receive all that was happening.

Author's Note: *As I relive this part of my life, I am able to reflect that magic can happen, and at this very moment I am affirming that there will be more magic in my life, but we will now get back to this story.*

Something I found to be most interesting was whenever I looked into taking more classes in my new-found career, the strangest things kept happening. Every class I signed up for was canceled or was already full.

Book One
Part I

I finally understood that for some reason it was not in my grand plan to take more massage classes, so I just stopped trying. I wasn't sure what would unfold next but I knew there was more to come; I just needed to be patient and allow the process to unfold.

Author's Note: *I know now that when I am doing any of my healing work it comes from an ancient knowing and awareness deep within me. These are my natural abilities; part of my "Cosmic Consciousness" and traditional education can sometimes repress and get in the way of our natural gifts.*

Then the early stages of my massage practice, a client asked me to go with her to a re–birthing workshop to support her in her process. At the time, I was not familiar with re–birthing, but I agreed to go with her and assist her. Re–birthing, as I was soon to find out, is a remarkable process, which we will discuss later. Not long into the session, after observing the work I was doing with my client, the facilitator of this workshop asked me if I would be interested in getting certified in breath work. She was beginning a certification class in two weeks and wanted to do a trade with me in exchange for a breath-work certification. I would give massages to her as well as the other people enrolled in the class in exchange for the tuition. Amazing isn't it? I was looking to expand my abilities and here was my opportunity. Without even thinking, I jumped at the chance to take this course. On a higher level, I was acutely aware that spirit was guiding my path.

As I mentioned earlier, when I was approached with this offer I did not have much knowledge about the practice of re-birthing and conscious breathing, but I was going to soon find out. I was a bit apprehensive but at the same time excited about learning the re-birthing process.

Initially, I was surprised that this was not a weekend workshop; this was a nine-month certification course, a huge commitment for me. At that juncture in my life I was a person who hesitated when making long-term commitments, yet I instinctively knew this was the perfect next step.

There is far more to the practice of breathing than one might imagine. I vaguely understood that breath is our life force energy, but after taking this certification course that vague understanding took on more meaning. Breath is vital to us, but how many people are conscious of their breath? For me one of the biggest revelations was to become conscious of how often I was holding my breath to keep from feeling a situation. It was alarming. More importantly, this is something the masses do without even being aware. Most of us live our daily lives using only shallow breathing. Yet oxygen is necessary for our survival. Oxygen is a major component in how our tissues grow and reproduce. When we exhale we exhale carbon dioxide, which is essential for plants and trees. Breath is vital to our existence. Breath is not only important to our physical growth but can be utilized to enhance our spiritual growth.

I quickly realized that breath–work would be a wonderful complement to the work I was doing with massage not to mention my own personal journey. It was during the course of my certification in breath–work that another doorway opened.

Book One
Part I

Chapter 8

It seemed as if the path I was walking on this time was blessed and I was on my way to engaging in my true purpose. Everything was falling into place without any effort. Then I was thrown another curve ball. At the age of forty-five I met Tom Kenyon, a sound healer, a musician and an overall a beautiful being. I met him when I attended one of his workshops. Actually, this was one of the first workshops I'd ever attended. The night before the workshop began, he always gave a free lecture, and before his lecture started I received a message. It was like there was a voice in my head talking to me. This intuitional guidance told me that Tom had a message for me; yet it took some time—perhaps three years for me to realize what that message was. That message would change my world and my perspective yet again. Having said this, I'd like to continue with my life changing encounter with Tom.

The first time I met Tom, I didn't recognize him, which always amazes me whenever I think about it, because I usually recognize people who I am spiritually connected to. I had met Tom some months earlier at a meeting about land in New Mexico. At the time, I was nursing a rather severe cut on my shin from a swimming accident, and Tom's presence seemed to get lost in the woodwork. So, when I went to this workshop and got this message about Tom having information for me I was totally unaware of my previous encounter. It was sometime later that a mutual friend reminded me that I had sat next to Tom several months before I attended the workshop. Whenever I think about that time in my life I always have the same puzzled confusion about not recognizing him when we first met. He was actually sitting right next to me and I didn't recognize him! That all changed once I listened to his voice. I instantly knew Tom was a part of my soul fabric. I always enjoy meeting people from my soul family here on earth, and this was no exception. I felt and still feel very blessed by my association with Tom, and I am absolutely delighted that I got to work with him in a very unique way, for you see Tom honored me by giving me the opportunity to give chair massages to his workshop attendees at many of his events between 1994 and 1997. This was a blessing because it allowed me to experience the joy of Tom's sound work and be activated at the same time.

This opportunity came to me quite by chance, or was it through divine intervention? After my first experience at Tom's workshop I was excited to attend the next workshop he was doing. It was the "Missing Years of Christ". As my resources were still in the growing stages, I wasn't able to pay for the workshop, so I asked the event coordinator if there was any way I could do a trade with Tom. Tom agreed, but said he'd prefer to have gift certificates for massages verses receiving the massage. So, being the bold person that I am, I suggested he give my services as a gift to the attendees of his workshop, and he agreed. In my humble opinion, it was like a marriage made in heaven. The kind of work I do was very complimentary to the work Tom was doing, so it was logical in my mind for it to continue. Being able to do this work with Tom is still beyond my ability to adequately express in words, but the Gods were shining on me as Tom and I made an arrangement to continue trading massage for my attendance at his events. I was the most blessed being on the planet, I was able to do my work, which I love, and I was doing it in this magical environment, and all the while I was continually being exposed to Tom's sound work with the crystal bowls.

For those of you who have never attended a workshop with Tom, he does sound work with bowls made of crystal throughout his workshops. The workshops were very experiential and captivating. It was through my attendance at Tom's workshops that my power of sound, which I work with today, was activated. Those years between 1994 and 1997 were pivotal years for me. I was laying a foundation for what was coming next.

Life is ever changing though, and relationships come and go. Sometimes they grow and sometimes they end. Sometimes we are not always ready when the shifts in our relationships take place. I know I wasn't ready for the end of my relationship with Tom. I remember the moment I realized that I would not be working with Tom again. It was after the conference that I attended in Bali in August of 1997. The awareness hit me square in my solar plexus. I would not be working in this way with Tom again. The sadness that accompanied this awareness was monumental and lived with me for many months, but it was time for me to move forward on my own. To this day I still have a wish to work with Tom again, but this time I'd like to work with him as his peer, blending the male and female energy of sound as we have done so many times in other dimensions and incarnations. Who knows, we are both on this planet, perhaps that wish will come true.

Time to Be ALIVE

Book One
Part I

Chapter 9

Once I was activated, no matter how much I yearned to stay connected to Tom, as he was a familiar essence or vibration for me on this planet, it was clearly not meant to be. I had to learn to fly alone so to speak. It was time to bring my gifts into the world.

Author's Note: *Remember what I shared with you earlier in the book about being in awe of other peoples' abilities? At the same time I also acknowledged that deep within, I knew I had the knowledge. Well the time was here for me to fess up to that and to own my wisdom, my awareness, my own "Spark of the Divine", my Cosmic Consciousness. What I had intuited many years before was true; within me lived the knowing, within each of us lives the knowing. I just needed to be opened to it. The tools of activation came to me through breath and sound, and since then I've been consciously opening to the power that lives within me and the possibilities of who I am as a spirit. I have expanded beyond my imagination, and I am continually being stimulated by interesting life experiences. I have also been exposed and have had to come face to face with the darkest energies within myself. Everyday I am faced with my darker self as well as my light. Everyday I am being challenged with decisions, decisions that define me. Everyday it happens, and some days I shine and some days I falter. I've realized it's a package deal this planet, which I will share with you as we continue, but for now we'll carry on.*

Time to Be ALIVE

Book One

Part II
Gurus, Guides and Masters

Chapter 1

Initially, once my deep creative energy was unleashed it seemed to ooze from my every pore. I was becoming more and more conscious of who and what I am. I was opening like a flower, and the energy unfolding was almost palpable.

Author's Note: *People very often marvel at the creativity which flows through me with such ease, but I am here to tell you within every person lives that same magic, for each and every one of us is a "Spark of the Divine". The "Cosmic Consciousness" naturally flows through us. You have your own magic living within you. It is time now, for every person to recognize who they truly are. To open yourself to your own creative forces and to recognize the immense power that lives within you.*

Since making the choice to walk my spiritual path, and when I say that what I am really attempting to convey is; once I decided to recognize and embrace the knowledge that I am spirit, and be honest with myself in my awareness that I am a "Spark of the Divine" many wondrous experiences began to unfold in my life, so many that in this writing I do not have the time nor do I have the patience to record them all in writing, for the myriad of experiences need another book. However I do want to share some of them as I feel they have been most important in relationship to my spiritual unfolding as well as to introduce to you my "spirit" guides.

Book One
Part II

Chapter 2

During this time it seemed everyone I knew who was on a spiritual path had a "spiritual guru"; some enlightened being that they studied with, and if they did not have a "spiritual guru" they had read volumes of books that gave them vast amounts of useful information. Since about the age of thirty I had stopped reading most books, for I was fairly certain I wasn't going to find my answers in reading. I've always been a doer, so reading just didn't seem the way for me to go, but I did imagine I'd have a master/teacher that would be of human form to give me guidance. I would like to stress this point; "I did imagine" because my imagination sometimes gets me in trouble. Sometimes my imagination becomes more like an agenda.

Author's Note: *Do any of you ever find that you get in your own way by having an agenda? I believe "imagine" at certain times just might qualify as an agenda, and agenda's can limit the opportunity of the "pure" imagination. What I am attempting to convey here is to be careful not to turn your imagination into an agenda, because agendas can and will stifle the freedom of creation. Anyway, I kept waiting for one to show up, but as it frequently happens in life, it didn't turn out that way. Do you think having "an agenda" got in the way of the process? Perhaps it slow things down a bit, but my teachers were finally shown to me, but not in the way I had expected. The one thing that can happen when you have an agenda is that you can miss the opportunities presented to you by having a limited imagination.*

Time to Be ALIVE

So I'm going forward on what I consider to be my spiritual path, all the while wondering when my guru/master would appear and take me under their wing, and work with me, imbuing me with all sorts of spiritual wisdom. Was I in for a major surprise!

Author's Note: *At this time I want to acknowledge that in the course of my life I have been blessed with many messengers, Tom Kenyon being one of them, and he has my deepest respect for awakening me to my abilities as a sound healer, but I didn't really look at Tom as being my spiritual "guru", although it was through my association with Tom I became acquainted with the beings I have come to know as my "spiritual gurus" or guides.*

In December of 1995 I had my first "conscious" encounter with star beings. It was in Hawaii at a Tom Kenyon workshop. It was about 4:00 am in Kona, on the Big Island of Hawaii. Because I couldn't sleep I was sitting in the hot tub, with the ocean just yards away from me and I decided to use this time to star gaze, a pastime of which I never tire. I have always felt a strong connection with the stars and planets. For some reason I have always felt they were a part of me, so whenever I get the chance to gaze at the heavens without all the city lights distracting the view I do so. While watching the stars, I observed something out of the ordinary. There in the heavens above were a series of lights that formed a familiar pattern. As I continued to observe I knew I had seen the pattern before but it took me six years to realize what this pattern was.

Author's Note: *The lights were in a pattern of the Kabbalah's Tree of Life—a symbol we had used in our Tarot study group.*

Book One
Part II

When I saw the lights I was dumbfounded at first, but I was more curious than alarmed or afraid. The lights were pulsating, and once I got over my initial shock, or better said surprise, I understood in a deep visceral way that the lights were communicating with me. I just knew these star beings were here for me. Even though I could not articulate the messages being sent to me I was very aware that I could understand the messages subconsciously if not consciously. I knew they were downloading information to me while at the same time connecting with me. I could feel they were healing me and bringing a yet to be realized wholeness to me, as well as a deeper connection with the all.

There were laser beams going from one light to another as if the laser beam was activating each individual light, and through that process information was being transmitted to me. It was amazing. I remember feeling totally in awe and so very blessed by this encounter.

I wondered if this was a one-time encounter of if I would be able to have the experience again? I went to the hot tub every night that I was in Kona, and every night they were there, and I was blessed each night to receive the information they were giving me. I knew they were preparing me and working with me for whatever lay in store for me. Since that moment forward I have been conscious of beings from other dimensions downloading information to me. The operative word here is conscious, for I feel these beings had always been there, it's just that now I was aware of them. Once I became aware of them I can honestly say I know their presence in my life is and always has been for my highest and best interest. I know they are supporting me in the work I am here on this planet to do. Finally I was becoming conscious of my guides. There were many more surprises in store for me, and my encounter with the star beings was just the tip of the iceberg.

Chapter 3

After the trip to Hawaii, I began to travel to many of the sacred sites around the world. Hawaii was the kick off for what lay ahead. I have always felt there was a pattern to these trips, in the way they unfolded in my life, because the sacred sites hold ancient knowledge and wisdom for me as well as everyone else to receive. Hawaii was just the beginning of this leg of my journey.

I have always thought it interesting that prior to my Hawaii adventure I had never had a passport, I had never needed one, nor had I ever imagined needing one. I had never traveled outside the country except to Canada, Baja, Mexico and the Caribbean, and at that time (remember those good old days) passports were not required. I also don't remember dreaming about traveling when I was young except I had always felt a resonance with Greece and the Middle Eastern countries, but beyond that it just wasn't in my realm of imagination to travel. I guess I felt I'd experience other places by reading or through pictures. Little did I know the adventures that were in store for me!

After I became exposed to the sound, and then the magical lights in the sky, which, as you know, I considered to be "star beings", my awareness of who I am was magnified. I was remembering. To be more precise, I was becoming cognitively aware that "I Am Spirit". The more solid I was in my understanding, the more I could remember. The more I could remember who I am, the more information I could receive and that is when I began hearing about sacred sites. Prior to this I had been very sheltered in relationship to things outside of my actual physical space, but that was going to change. The world was opening up to me.

I need to go backward in time for a moment and share what I consider to be another piece of interesting information in my unfolding saga. Sometime in early 1995 I knew that I was going to need a passport, and the idea of that was very foreign to me, as I mentioned previously, but something inside of me was driving me to pursue this. I remember I got an application, and I had my passport photo taken but that is as far as it went. It would be more than a year before I would act on this.

On January 1st, 1997 I knew I had to stop procrastinating because I needed to get that passport and I needed to get it immediately. Since I had all the paper work completed I went to the local post office during the first week of January and I applied for my first passport. I didn't have any trips planned, nor was I thinking about taking any trips, yet I knew I was going to need a passport. At the time I was unaware of how soon I would be traveling abroad, but the opportunity came sooner than I ever thought possible.

Several weeks into January of 1997 a client/friend of mine who worked for Continental Airlines had put together a trip for a group who where going to Machu Picchu to do a ceremony there on February 12th. Because of the political unrest in Peru people had cancelled last minute and she found herself with these round trip tickets from San Francisco to Cusco, Peru for around $600.00. She made them available to me if I wanted them. There was one condition; I had only a short time to make my mind up. Wow, I'd never even imagined going to Machu Picchu, and it had only been in the last several years I had even heard of it, let alone had a desire to go. But here it was; airfare to one of the most well known sacred sites available and being offered to me.

Here was an opportunity or a doorway that was opening to me. What to do? Can you imagine my surprise? Can you imagine my hesitation? I had hesitation in buckets. Taking this trip meant I'd be traveling out of the country for the first time. I would be going to a country where I did not speak the language; did not know anyone; had no concept of where I would stay; and there was political unrest in Peru to boot. Also, I would not be traveling with the group nor did I know if I would even meet up with them. Wow again. After further investigation I found out that Machu Picchu was miles away from Cusco and I would need to take a train or helicopter from Cusco to Machu Picchu. Wow again. I went back and forth on this for several days, and time was getting shorter and shorter for me to make a decision. This was too much, I felt like I was on a roller coaster. On some level I knew this was an opportunity and I felt I was being called to go. I also understood this was not something I should pass up, but fear can be pervasive, persuasive and intrusive at times like these.

Finally I decided to surrender and turn it over to God, and if I was meant to go I'd get my passport in time, if not it was not meant to be. Well as you have probably guessed my passport arrived 3 days before I was scheduled to depart, so I was going. A friend came with me, which meant I would at least have a traveling companion to Lima. I would then be going alone to Cusco and Machu Picchu without hotel reservations, without knowing if I would meet up with this group and without speaking the language. I just took a leap of faith and went. Everything about the trip went smoothly from the moment I surrendered.

Author's Note: *I had the most amazing experiences, and it was the perfect place to begin my introduction to the sacred sites. I now understand that when you visit sacred sites there are vibrations of wisdom from the ancient ones that has been recorded in the stones that is available to us if we choose to receive it. The s(tones) do hold the knowing.*

I was only able to take time off from work for six days, and this was including my travel time, so I was limited in the number of adventures I could have in Peru and Machu Picchu, but I feel I got to experience the overall vibration that Machu Picchu holds within.

I would like to share a few of my experiences with you since this was my maiden voyage to a sacred site outside of the United States.

First I need to tell you I did meet up with the group, quite by accident in Agua Caliente, the little village where people stay when going to Machu Picchu. There was a woman from Lima and a man from Argentina traveling with the group and we connected on the bus going up to Machu Picchu. They were wonderful companions and both of them had visited Machu Picchu many times and were very familiar with it, so they became my guides. When we were going from place to place we would do ceremonies and give offerings to the God/Goddess. You can trust me when I tell you this was better than any guided tour I could have paid for. The God/Goddess was shining on me.

Book One
Part II

One of the most fascinating places for me was this large slanted stone I had seen several people lay down on. I followed course and lay down on this stone with my hands above my head and my feet spread eagle. I looked like I was making an angel in the snow as I laid on the rock. All the while I lay there I felt like it was the philosophers' stone, or at least my philosophers' stone.

While I lay there the sun was filling me with its infinite knowing while at the same time wisdom from the stone was penetrating me. I was immersed in the vibration of nature and the wisdom of the ancient ones. I felt like what seemed to be electricity flowing through me as I was being activated, and my vibrational field was being enhanced. It was an exhilarating experience; one I do not have words for, except to say, it was an unforgettable moment.

After leaving the stone, the couple I was exploring with saw this very spiritual and gentle man entering what appeared to be a cave. We went to the place where he disappeared and waited for him. Once he reappeared he knelt and touched the tears that were streaming down his cheeks with his fingers and then touched those fingers to the earth. My newfound friends directed me to form a circle around him, and he came to each of us and touched our hearts then our foreheads with his hand, in the fashion of a blessing. No words were spoken but it was a most moving experience to have with what some might call a "stranger".

After our blessing we decided to enter the cave. While inside we preformed a ceremony and gave offerings to mother earth. I noticed the rocks were weeping, and I touched the water seeping from the rock with my finger and then I tasted the wisdom of mother earth's nectar with my lips. Now we were joined. While I was in the cave it felt as if I was in the womb of the great mother being re-birthed. It was phenomenal. I was being birthed into another "new" spiritual adventure.

This began my travels abroad as well as a major downloading of information from each of the sacred sites. For you see; the sacred sites as well as the "star" beings became my "guru's". Not exactly how I imagined, but finally I became aware of my guides.

After Machu Picchu my spiritual odyssey took me to Bali, where I accompanied a group on a retreat with Tom Kenyon. We traveled to most of the island's sacred sites and temples, but for me Bali did not capture my heart the way Machu Picchu did. Bali was a more emotionally difficult trip for me as the energy there brought up many of my issues. I had to look at a lot of "stuff" during that trip that proved to be uncomfortable for me to come face to face with, and it had the added distinction of being the last time I would be working with Tom.

In September of 1998 my next journey took me to a Conference in the Yucatan. What can I tell you about Maya land? I had no idea what to expect when I decided to go. I thought the speakers were drawing me, but as it turned out it was the land and the wisdom within the land that I went to experience and it was magical for me. It turns out that I have some very strong spiritual ties to Central and South America.

While at the conference one of the speakers I met introduced me to the names of the Mayan Gods/Goddess. He ended his lecture with us chanting the names of the

Book One
Part II

Mayan Gods/Goddess. When we were finished I was awestruck. I had to go to my room just to process the experience. I felt the power in the phonetics of the names as we chanted them and I still work with them in my Sound Healing Meditations today.

Author's Note: *I feel strongly that I need to travel again to the Yucatan before 2012 with a group of people so that we can chant those names at the sacred sites. There is something very powerful in the tones of these names.*

The rest of 1998 was a quite but 1999 turned out to be a very busy travel year for me. It had not started out that way. Initially I was only booked to go to England for a crop circle symposium. I was going to be toning for the closing ceremony. Yet my trip to England was just one of many trips during 1999. Over time it became evident this was going to be the year for major growth for me.

My first journey of 1999 was to Mt. Shasta for the yearly Wesak celebration. I had scheduled to do massage at Wesak in 1998 unaware that I would be traveling to Egypt three days after the celebration. Upon realizing the time crunch I was going to be in, I did everything to cancel the trip to Mt Shasta, but I had made a commitment and I could not get out of it. As they say there are reasons for everything. While I was at Wesak, I met someone who turned out to be a partner of mine in another dimension, or if it's easier to understand, a partner in a past life. I needed to meet him and form a bond with him before I began my other travels, as we had work to do together.

Author's Note: *Wesak is the celebration of the Buddha Full Moon celebrated in late April or when the sun is in*

Time to Be ALIVE

Taurus. You can get more information about this by doing a search for "Wesak" on the internet.

After Wesak, I was on a plane to Egypt. Egypt was the last place I had planned to travel, but the opportunity to go on this trip happened quite by accident. It was an opportunity I could not refuse. Even though I already had arrangements to travel to England in July, Egypt became my next destination. When I found out about the trip in March I knew Egypt was calling me. I just knew intuitively something very important was going to happen during the Egypt trip.

Egypt is the "seat" of sound healing in my opinion, and it was my destiny to go. I knew in every fiber of my being that my "ancient" sound would be activated there. This intuition was confirmed by two other psychics while I was at Wesak. Both of them came to me telling me they had a message for me regarding my next journey. I can share with you that I fully expected to be hearing thunder and seeing bolts of lightening, but nothing like that happened. However I had the most incredible time while I was in Egypt. I was beginning to find out just how many sacred places I had connections to, for you see Egypt also felt like my home. While traveling to the various locations throughout Egypt I was aware I'd been there in many incarnations as the memories kept flooding in the whole time I was there. I had only one disappointment; my intuition had seemed to be wrong.

Again I was in for a surprise. About six months after my return from Egypt, I received a copy of a photo in the mail. One of the other attendees of the conference sent a photo she had taken of her sister while we were in the King's Chamber in the Great Pyramid. I'm in the sarcophagus toning with the crystal bowl, and in the photo she captured an Orb the size of a basketball above my head. It is interesting to note that this picture was taken before digital cameras. Yet there it was; an Orb on my crown chakra. It was a confirmation of my initial intuition. I knew it the minute I saw it. This was proof the spirits were reactivating my ancient sound abilities in the most amazing sound chamber on this planet.

In July of 1999 I went to England to explore crop circles, Stonehenge, Glastonbury, and Avebury. I was honored with the opportunity to do sound at the closing ceremonies of a crop circle symposium in Wiltshire. I had heard many things about crop circles and had marveled at the precision in which they seem to be made, but until you have been in a crop circle for yourself they are difficult to describe. Crop circles are a magical phenomena and being inside of one is a mind-altering experience. They are filled with energy, and if you are willing to receive it, they can open the vibrational fields within you. My suggestion is that you go and experience them for yourself as attempting to explain it could never do the experience justice.

I had so many mystical adventures in England, but I have chosen to share one with you.

It was our last day in England. I would be flying out the next morning, and my travel companion was driving on to Scotland. We visited our last crop circle that morning and I lost my only keepsake from my trip. I had purchased a Celtic pendant in Glastonbury and had decided to wear it that last day. After we came out of the crop circle, I discovered my pendant, not the chain, but the pendant was gone. I took off all my clothes looking for it and took everything out of the trunk of the car trying to find it and the pendant was nowhere. So logically I assumed I'd lost it in the crop circle, where it would be next to impossible to find. So my pendant would stay with the crop circle as an offering to the Gods.

We then went on to Avebury. In my humble opinion, Avebury is a major energy site, probably more powerful than Stonehenge, and after Avebury we went to Silbury Hill which is a man-made hill dating back to 2660BCE, and is made of 12,000 million cubic feet of chalk and earth, and is considered to be one of the earth mysteries that has various legends connected to it. In the car park at Silbury Hill I encountered a gentleman who for some reason had been attempting to get my attention since I had been in England. Because this is so important to the overall experience I think further explanation is warranted here, so please bear with me.

In the Wiltshire crop circle area, there is a place called "The Barge". It is a pub next to a canal, where the "croppies" met daily. When a new crop circle was discovered the location was indicated with a push pin on a map inside the pub to so people could head out from there to visit the crop circle. In the evening people gathered there to drink, dine and discuss the discoveries of the day. This same man who was now in the "car park" had been coming to me everyday at the Barge telling me he had to discuss something very important with me. I always dismissed him, telling him my friends were waiting for me and I didn't have time to talk. I must say he had been persistent, but for some reason I was resisting whatever he wanted to share with me, so to this point I had been successful in dodging the conversation.

Book One
Part II

But here he was walking over to me in the car park. We literally pulled into the car park at the same moment. It was uncanny, what were the odds? I couldn't hide because there I was in plain sight and it was obvious he had seen me and was walking directly towards me. This time I had no choice, I was caught and I was going to listen. He began again telling me he had something important he needed to discuss with me. He asked me if I would be in England for the eclipse, which was happening in August. This was going to be the last eclipse of the century, so there was a lot of interest surrounding it. As this was the middle of July, I told him I would not be here for the eclipse and I was leaving in the morning. He asked me if it would be possible for me to stay. I look at him incredulously and told him that it would not be possible for me to stay, as I had to return home to work. He then inquired if I could come back for the eclipse. Now with some frustration arising I explained to him I did not have the financial resources to return to England in such a short time. He went on to tell me how very important it was that I be in England during the eclipse. He further went on to explain that because of the eclipse it was time for the Mary/Michael lines to be opened and my energy was necessary for this. Needless to say I thought this was absurd, and he was a little crazy. I went on to tell him I did not have any idea what Mary/Michael lines were, but I assured him that there would be thousands of people there during the eclipse and I was sure there would be a great deal of amazing energy around to support the Mary/Michael lines opening, so I didn't feel my energy would be missed. He became insistent at this point explaining that it was my energy that was necessary.

He also explained that the Mary/Michael lines were male/female energy lines that circled the earth and at certain points they crossed (somewhat like DNA strands) and where they crossed were power energy points. Silbury Hill as it happens is a point where the lines crossed. I was still dumbfounded by what he was suggesting. Why would my energy be necessary? Anyway after several more attempts to convince me to either stay or return he requested that I bury something of mine on top of Silbury Hill so that my energy would be there. I agreed to do this but told him that I had nothing with me I could bury. That morning I had the pendant, but now I had nothing. He then asked if he gave me a crystal would I bury it and take a crystal home and meditate with that crystal on the day and time of the eclipse. Of course I agreed to do that. So I went to his car where he just happened to have crystals in his trunk, and chose two crystals, one to bury and one to take home. My travel companion asked if he could have a crystal to bury with me. After we choose the crystals this gentleman got into his car and left.

Author's Note: *I never saw this man again, and felt it odd that he appeared at the moment we drove in and left once he had delivered the information to me. I have always wondered if he was another avatar appearing in my life to give me guidance.*

However this is not the end of the story. It gets better. My travel companion and I climbed Silbury Hill to bury the crystals and to do a ceremony with the crystal bowl. At the top of the hill I picked up a stick to help me dig a hole. Silbury Hill is very hard-packed earth and chalk, so digging is not so easy, but when I stuck the stick in the ground to begin digging, a hole opened up, and I dropped the crystal down. I then started the ceremony with the

Book One
Part II

sound, while my travel companion was still trying to dig a hole to bury his crystal. After the ceremony I was picking up my crystal bowl and blanket, and there on the ground several feet from the buried crystal was the pendant I had lost that morning. Well, can you imagine how startled I was! I knew this was a message, a very impressive message, and I decided right then and there I would be traveling back to England for the eclipse.

I came back to England the following month to do work with the Mary/Michael lines. It was a very different trip with very different experiences. This time I was on a mission. I came with the male friend from Australia who I had met at Wesak in Mt Shasta. Prior to my first trip to England we had been doing sound ceremonies at the sacred sites in Mt Shasta. Unbeknownst to us the Mary/Michael lines also run through Mt Shasta. We had been working with the Mary/Michael lines without knowing it, so who better to continue that work with, than my friend from Australia.

We got a book telling us where the lines crossed, and we did toning at all those points until the day before the eclipse, and on that day we finished our work at the top of Silbury Hill. The day of the eclipse our journey came to its end in Glastonbury, where I toned at an eclipse ceremony. We had many wonderful adventures during the 10 days we spent in England doing our work. It was one of those "beyond belief" experiences.

Author's Note: *I found out 4 years later that approximately 6 months after the eclipse, Silbury Hill caved in at the top, and what they refer to as a sinkhole now exists. They have fenced the area off with barbwire fencing to keep the tourists away. So what do you think? Did we open the energy?*

Much to my delight that was not my last trip of 1999, there were two more trips in store for me. In September of that year I traveled to Australia, for a conference. The trip was brief, but I had met a lot of people while I was there so I decided another trip was in order, only this trip would be longer. I had decided to do a two-month spiritual sojourn there, so I returned to Australia in December only to be deported to New Zealand, which we will discuss later.

Author's Note: I know my travels are not over, in fact in 2003, I went to France and I have a trip planned for Ireland as well as another journey to the Yucatan.

As I said before, there are far too many adventures to share them in this book, perhaps I'll write another book at another time, but for the moment, it is clear that all these ancient sites are linked in some way, some stronger than others, but linked all the same, and in turn my spiritual unfolding was some how linked to their power and ancient wisdom.

As you have read, between 1996 and 2000 it seemed as if I was on a crash course downloading and activating information. The picture in the King's Chamber is a visual example of this process. What a blessing that this process was visually recorded; for sometimes it is still hard for me to believe all that has happen, so the picture is my proof. During this time all of my studies with Astrology, Tarot, Numerology and The I Ch'ing were being fortified and my deeper wisdom more available then before.

Book One
Part II

Author's Note: The star beings continued to download information, and at the writing of this book still do. My channels are still being opened and the veils were and still are lifting. Even through all of this, through all the spiritual experiences and revelations, still to this day, even though my channels are open, I can get lost in the illusion of this planet. I can get lost in the minutia. It's almost as if the more open I become, the more vulnerable I am. I am still learning how to handle my ever changing vibration in this dimension, as well as share the amazing gifts I have accessed. We will discuss this more latter, but for now we will continue with the journey for there is much more to share.

Time to Be ALIVE

Book One

Part III
Deported or Imported?

Chapter 1

On December 31, 1999 the stars were aligning in a powerful way with my own natal chart. For those of you who understand astrology, in my natal chart, my Chiron and Ascendant are conjunct in Sagittarius. Transiting Pluto and Chiron were conjunct and were then conjuncting my Chiron and Ascendant. Now Pluto and Chiron only cross paths every 70-80 years, and this is considered an astrological rarity, as well as a powerful conjunction. Chiron is the wounded healer, and Pluto is the transformational planet, so in honor of this momentous astrological event occurring in my chart, I decided to go on a two month spiritual journey to Australia, which by a twist of fate and some serious "God-like" intervention turned out to be in New Zealand instead. That alone should give you some indication of how powerful this trip was going to be.

As I mentioned before the trip was meant to take place in Australia but when I arrived in Australia there was a technical glitch and I was deported and sent to New Zealand. I knew the minute I was taken to the internment room that the Hands of God were at work, so I just needed to surrender.

Author's Note: *Does anyone notice a pattern here with surrender? Surrender seems to be something I'm working on this lifetime.*

Time to Be ALIVE

My New Zealand trip was one of the most interesting experiences thus far especially because of the circumstances of how I got there. New Zealand opened me to the promise of the new millennium while taking me on an incredible spiritual odyssey. Being deported is a traumatic experience, yet when I arrived in New Zealand, the country, as well as the people, opened their arms to me, nurtured me, and embraced me. They made me feel at home as well as at ease. New Zealand is a very unique and special place—one I would love to be able to experience again and again.

I see New Zealand as being an archetype of a union. Here you have two islands, which vibrate differently, co-existing as one identity. The North Island has semi-tropical areas, while the South Island has glaciers. It is without a doubt one of the most beautiful countries and well worth the time, energy and money to visit, but for me there was great spiritual significance to this country. By now you may be aware that I'm very sensitive to vibrations, and New Zealand was no exception. The North Island felt very Lemurian and heart centered and the South Island very Atlantian with a rugged energy and filled with a certain survival orientation and more in the vibration of the lower chakras, as well as a cerebral orientation. Yet they energetically co-existed as one in a beautiful way.

If felt to me as if divine spirit decided I had to experience the vibration of New Zealand for myself. The new millennium was heralding in the time for union, and as I mentioned earlier New Zealand in my opinion is the archetype of union. This was confirmed with each day of my time in New Zealand. The vibrations of both islands were rich and flowing, and seemed to be less encumbered than other places I have traveled. It felt as if there was a unique and unrefined purity to this amazing land. For some reason, I needed to feel it, and absorb it for myself, probably so I could support that process of union in my own life as well as support it in other peoples' lives. After all, now is the time for us to bring the heart and mind together for us to collaborate individually while as one. Now is the time to take ourselves back to a less encumbered yet pure existence. New Zealand holds the archetype to what seems almost like a place before time.

There were several places in New Zealand that I experienced timelessness. Several times I was knocked over by the experiences. I would have to stop and regroup for several days so that I could process the energy and vibrations. It was so subtle, yet so very powerful! It is impossible to isolate one or two experiences for the entire time I was in New Zealand was the experience.

Author's Note: *Union is an important component to the overall theme of this book. This is the time we need to recognize our Oneness. Even though we appear to be separate we are ONE. Just as the North and South Island of New Zealand are physically separated by water, they are still one. Even though they vibrate differently, within those vibrations exist the All. As I mentioned above, I am certain experiencing these vibrations was important for my own personal journey as well as being able to share this awareness with others.*

Again I felt my life was turning in another direction. It wasn't a 180° turn, it was more like a curve or 90° shift, but things definitely shifted. During the period between 2000 when I returned from New Zealand and through to the present (2009), many things have happened that have had profound effects on my psyche and my spirituality.

Book One

Part IV
Back to Reality and Into Despair

Chapter 1

After my return from New Zealand I felt very strongly that I needed to go on the road and touch people, so I gave up everything, sold my furniture and moved into a camper–van and started traveling around the country with the Bay Area as my base. I got married and divorced to a man I met in New Zealand and I had what I would call a long dark night of the soul experience. This all began with my "Chiron return", December 31, 1999 and continued for a little over seven years.

Author's Note: *I strongly believe that astrology is a wonderful mirror into the past, present and future. At 50 every person experiences a Chiron Return because it takes 50 years for Chiron to orbit the earth. The experiences this transit will lead you through will depend on which house your Chiron is in. The outer planets such as Saturn, Jupiter, Neptune, Uranus, Pluto (no longer considered a planet by science) and Chiron (which is technically not a planet) take a longer time to make their orbit around the Sun. The Earth, which takes one year, and the Moon orbits the earth in 28 days. Because of this the outer planets generally have a strong impact on a person's life because the cycles are longer and when there is an aspect the effects of a transit last for a longer period of time. If you have an interest in astrology there are many wonderful books, but I would strongly suggest that you get your chart done and then find a good teacher to take classes with. It will be very insightful for your life process and can assist you in finding your life path.*

Let us get back to my return to reality. In the year 2000, to mark my Chiron return, I experienced a spider bite, not just any spider bite; it was a Brown Recluse spider bite, whose poison is often deadly. I was bitten September of 2000 and did not realize the bite was poisonous for seven months thereafter. All the while I kept getting sicker and sicker as the poison infiltrated my whole system. Fortunately I was very healthy when the bite occurred; had I not been in good physical shape, most likely it would have killed me. It affected all the organs and systems in my body. I gained at least 80 lbs within three months as my body was building adipose or fat to help absorb the poison. My body was doing everything it could to save me, but the bite placed an enormous stress on my nervous system, my endocrine system, and respiratory system not to mention my heart, kidneys and liver. In essence my whole physical body was affected. Somehow I survived, and I know I will be healthy and wholesome again, yet I am still experiencing and adjusting to the aftermath of the bite. To this day it continues to influence my life and it still has its effects on me. I also admit that after 8 years I am still learning to embrace the experience.

Needless to say the spider bite was life altering and seemed to unravel my idyllic life, but there seemed to be more going on. I have gone through many challenges in my life, but nothing as profound as this. After my return from New Zealand my life seemed to spiral out of control. Every choice I made seemed to lead me in the wrong direction. Every instinct seemed to be riddled with confusion. Each and every one of my insecurities were being stimulated, and I was reeling in an emotional cesspool.

My marriage and the ending of my marriage also influenced my world and created a great upheaval producing even more strife for me to deal with. It was a deeply emotional experience for me. Without going into detail, the relationship seemed to tear my heart apart, spiritually and emotionally. This had a profound effect on me and I feel it contributed greatly to my dark night of the soul experience.

Author's Note: *As I see this in hindsight I feel that for me to progress further as a spiritual being, my world had to be stripped away from me, and as you will see I almost didn't have the spiritual fortitude to endure it.*

Time to Be ALIVE

Book One
Part IV

Chapter 2

Author's Note: *I am going to share my "dark night" experience with you, however I will tell it from the present time perspective. This is the only way I believe I can relive it, as I am still healing from it. So I hope this doesn't create a lot of confusion to those who are reading it.*

It is now 2008, and I have not yet released the weight, and I have spent a lot of time doing cleansings and coping with all the changes that have been going on in my body. In addition to dealing with the results of the spider bite I began menopause in 2005. It is interesting to go through this physical change. I have always loved my menses, and the cleansing that it brought to my life. I experienced losing it an extreme loss and because of this, it felt as if something vital had been stripped from me. It became more of an emotional loss for me than a natural physiological process. So I have been going through a lot. I've been challenged mentally, emotionally and spiritually as well as financially. My healing practice began to slow down and continued to decline year by year until it was nearly obsolete. As each year passed from 2000 to 2007 life became darker and darker. I applied every spiritual principle I knew, and yet the darkness continued to envelop me. I had massive confusion, and as each year passed and nothing seemed to be changing there came a point where I had a total lack of faith. It was the deepest sense of abandonment I had ever known. I felt lost. Whatever wisdom I had absorbed over the years seemed to make no difference. My usual thought process and my ability to create just was not working during this time. I was sinking into oblivion and in the end all I could feel was nothing!

Time to Be ALIVE

People talk about depression, but this went beyond depression, it went to the core of my being. I don't ever in my adult awareness remember having reached such apathy prior to this. In the past I have had many bouts with depression, especially in my early years, but I had never reached these depths. I had known desperation, and the desire to leave the planet. I have had a sense of being lost and abandoned, but never like this. I was a zombie going through the motions of living. Before my descent into apathy, I had a deep anger, and then a massive confusion took hold. I felt betrayed and then I felt nothing. I had an overwhelming desire to exit the planet, so much so I was actually creating it.

I was literally out of my body, and observing myself, but I was conscious of what my body was feeling. I felt myself dying on a cellular level and I watched myself going through the motions of living. I was just existing. Actually it was less than existing.

I felt my body's tissues breaking down. Even during the early months of the spider bite I had never felt my body dying, although I had been close to it but spiritually it was nothing like this. This was deep and to the core. Not only was my body deteriorating at an accelerated rate, but a part of me wanted to let it happen, and there was a part of me that did not care if it happened. I had lost my desire as well as my passion. Somewhere deep inside of me I knew that if I were going to survive I needed to regain my passion for life again or I was going to die. I had lost the heart to live, figuratively and literally.

By the time I slipped into my darkest hours, and was in financial despair a dear friend took me in. I did my best to hide my internal upheaval, but people who are tuned in energetically feel what's happening even when we attempt to hide what we are feeling. It got to such a point that my friend with whom I was staying was so worried she wanted me to go to the hospital or a doctor, but I knew that even though it was my body that was being affected, it was my heart that had to change. I assured her that a doctor would not be able to help me through this. I knew that no medical doctor or medicine in the world could help me unless I could summon up the courage to help myself.

It shattered me even more to realize I was hurting people who loved me. I wished I could go crawl in a hole and just fade away, but I couldn't summon the strength to do that either. I knew my purpose on this planet was not to cause others unnecessary pain yet I felt I was doing just that. I was in a catch-22 situation. I needed a place to live, and because of my friend's kindness she was watching me implode. I was conscious of this, and felt even more destroyed by this. I just didn't know how to pull myself out of the mire.

During this dark period I lost trust within myself. Everything that I knew and understood about why I was on this planet was being challenged. I felt perhaps I had fulfilled my purpose here, or had totally misunderstood what my purpose was.

There was a point I felt I had lost the universal force that supported me on this planet. You see I had always felt the universal force working with me. The first part of this book is a clear example of how blest I'd been up until this point. Somehow in the past several years whatever magic I possessed seemed to be gone. Still, I kept plodding along until it came to the point I just didn't know who I was anymore nor did I know exactly what my purpose for being here was. The world I was living in now was not a world I knew, and it wasn't a world I recognized. My life and my existence felt very bleak.

If that was not bad enough, to top it off the IRS, an organization whose tactics I strongly disagree with was after me. I just did not feel I had the fortitude to deal with these horrendous weights that kept falling on me. The faith that had always comforted me seemed to be gone. It somehow had slowly drained from me. I couldn't find my strength, my inner strength to pull through this. Somewhere along the way I gave up mentally, emotionally, physically but most of all spiritually.

My channels were still open and my veils still lifted, so I could feel the negative shifting in the world's economical and politically arenas. I started feeling the shifts in the year 2000 and then September 11, 2001 happened and these sensations became even more intense as each year passed. I felt these shifts deep within me and felt helpless because I had no defenses left to fight against it or to remain positive, or direct my energy in a positive way. I really didn't have words to articulate to others what was happening within me, so I felt even more remote and lost as each year passed. At the time I had neither children nor husband nor lover to bind me to this planet, so I didn't have that motivation to rally me and I was having a tough time rallying myself. Every time I conjured the energy to rally myself it seemed I'd fall flat on my face. Each time this happened it seemed to fortify my sense of helplessness. I just wanted it to end. I knew that I was loved and I am loved by many people. I have been so blessed in this lifetime for I have touched so many people and I have been touched by so many people that I know I am a loved being, but that still wasn't enough for me to choose to go on. I was in a place of hopeless despair.

Hindsight is so wonderful because you get to see the reality from eyes that are not clouded by the trauma of the situation you have just passed through. I now realize that in fact some power was taking care of me because other work came to me. It wasn't healing work, but I had the means to create resources for myself. When my resources were so low I could not afford a place to live a friend gave me a place to live, and I will be forever grateful for that. Yet I tell you this in hindsight for during those dark years, I was not able to see my blessings as I do now.

Time to Be ALIVE

Book One

Part V
Re-awakening

Chapter 1

Acknowledging this spiritual break-down to the world is one of the most difficult things I have ever done. My ego is having a challenge with my dark night of the soul revelation. To be so exposed is very unsettling, but I understand that it is a part of who I am, and I need to be able to share the good as well as the ugly. So I shall continue with the saga. Since I am writing this after the fact it is obvious that I somehow summoned the strength to survive this.

I remember my turning point clearly. I had a client/friend, who was an amazing being. At times I wondered why he worked with me because he understood this universe and was not in any spiritual need. He was more of an example to me. I remember as if it were yesterday the second to last session I had with him. I was toning into his crown chakra, (this is part of my healing work) and I felt all of our barriers dissolve and we became as one. It was one of the most pristine moments I have ever experienced during a toning session.

"L" and I often had philosophical discussions. He was wonderful to talk with. He had great wisdom, and even more importantly a clear understanding of detachment. He was able to experience life without the attachments that seem to bog most of us down. He was very Zen–like.

He always encouraged my work with sound. I had great respect for "L" and his encouragement meant a lot to me.

"L" was his ninety–eight year old father's caretaker and I felt it was his dad that bound "L" to this planet which turned out to be true. The day his father died, and was taken to the mortuary "L" drove him self to the hospital and was diagnosed and admitted with leukemia. His immune system was shot and the doctors gave him less than a week to live.

He was helping me with my taxes, so he sent me an email to let me know his condition, and made a point of telling me he was listening to my CD's every night. As I mentioned earlier he had always felt my sound was very powerful. He once told me all the years of mediation he had done could not take him to the place my sound was able to carry him in just a blink of an eye.

He lived for another two months. In November 2007, a month after he entered the hospital I had the opportunity to talk with him. He told me how the doctors were amazed but also perplexed that he was doing so well. He continued to tell me that was because they didn't know about his secret weapon. I asked him what that was, and was surprised to hear him say his secret weapon was my CDs, and he told me again that he listened to them every night. What a powerful thing for me to hear and from someone I respected so much. It became very clear to me then. I knew that "L" was going to leave the planet, but before he could go he had to make sure I understood I still had work to do. When I got off the phone I broke down in tears, but they were not tears of despair they were tears of gratitude. I still cannot relate this story without tears coming to my eyes. Even though he has crossed he left his mark.

That conversation did its work, for I understood that I still had more to give this planet; I knew it was not yet time for me to go. I felt it on a visceral level, and knew that I had to reverse any damage I might have done during this dark night of the soul experience. I needed to accept as well as surrender to the situation I was in and summon up my trust and faith. I needed to recognize once again that there is a universal timing to everything. My ego-self was not in control, my higher self was and I could no longer operate on my ego's agenda. I needed to surrender all the way, not just an inch, not just a mile, but to the very tips of my toes and beyond. I needed to surrender and allow the divine process to unfold. "L" had reminded me that the gift of sound that I bring to this world is powerful, and still needs to be heard, and some how the universal force will find a way for it to be heard, and those that need to experience it will experience it, I just need to be available to share it.

Author's Note: *Surrender has come up a lot during writing this, and it is a pivotal component to a stable and enduring spiritual reality for me. We will discuss this more latter, but for now as you read ponder on what surrender means to you.*

I am now just beginning to come back fully into my power, enough so that I am writing this book. I am certain it was not an accident that it was a spider bite that started this process of unraveling and recommitment because of what the spider symbolizes. I am sure most of you know that grandmother spider is a very powerful totem in the Native American culture for she weaves the bridge between the worlds and this was my second poisonous spider bite in one lifetime. I have been told that if you survive a poisonous spider bite it is considered great medicine. For me there are no coincidences, for this second spider bite was the beginning of a seven year saga that nearly cost me my life, physically and spiritually. The "spider" and its symbolic inference now have great significance to me and it has definitely made an impression.

My marriage and its eventual break up which was occurring at the same time was part of my unraveling, part of the process. The spider bite had a physical effect on my body which affected me emotionally, while the relationship had an emotional effect on me which affected my physical being. Releasing the resentment and anger that my body is carrying as well as bringing my spiritual being into sync with my physical/emotional body is a process that I am still engaged with. As my process moves forward, I am also still very aware of the shifts that are occurring on the planet, and the impact that it is having on people. I have been feeling it for the last 8 years. We are definitely a planet in flux. Since it is obvious I have been having my own personal experience with "being in flux", I'm wondering; does my process of "being in flux" play a part in the overall scheme of things? Was my time in the darkness preparing me for what is to come? Is "Being in flux" another issue that this book seems to be going towards? The fact that this book is still forming as I write seems significant, for I have no consciousness of where it is going. My guess is that it is something we are probably meant to explore together so it is best that I continue writing and we shall see where it goes.

Book One
Re-awakening

Chapter 2

During what I refer to as my dark night of the soul experience several people asked me to consider whether there might be other negative forces that were contributing to my breakdown, i.e. energy forces attempting to suppress me, and my gifts of healing and sound. They felt that many of the experiences that drove me to my desperation were a means of energetically stopping me and preventing me from bringing my gifts into the world. That was an interesting idea, for I had been aware of "other" energy forces on this planet for years, but I had always advocated the concept that we as spiritual beings have power, and when people are operating in their own power, other energy forces would not be able to penetrate their energy field.

Yet perhaps if the spirit is worn down enough, and you lose your center I imagine anything would be possible. I imagine if you are not shining your own light, darkness can come in. And what if one never recognizes they have power or consider themselves to be powerful? I imagine they could be susceptible to "other energy" forces interfering with their psyche. So after being asked to consider the possibilities of this, as well as having the experience of going through my darkest hour I decided to look at it and explore it in a way I had never done before. That exploration is something I will be sharing with you as the book progresses, and it is probably the main reason I am taking the time to share my thoughts with you in a public forum.

So for whatever the reason, maybe the spider bite, my relationship, other dark energy forces or something internal that sparked my "dark night of the soul experience", I have learned from it; I have been humbled by it; I have become stronger from the experience. In addition I know that the gifts I have to share with the world will be more powerful because of these experiences. From this experience I realize I have a story to tell and I have wisdom to share, so the next part of this book will reveal my deeper thoughts in a more philosophical and exploratory context.

Author's Note: *I will be shifting gears now and we will be looking at life in a more philosophical way with tidbits of my personal reality thrown in because it is through my lenses of experience that I have formed a philosophical perspective in the first place. It will be easier to follow because you now know a bit of my history.*

Book Two

Foreword

Philosophies, Explanations & Visions

As I already intimated, Book Two will be a more philosophical discussion which was spurred by the question posed to me by several people during my journey into darkness regarding "other" energy forces blocking me or preventing me from sharing my gifts. I cannot tell you that "other" energy forces were attempting to block my energy specifically, but it did begin a thought process in me that started unraveling some very interesting information that I have formulated and gathered over the years. It is my belief that our society has been manipulated over the course of hundreds of years. I do believe knowledge is repressed in our world. I also believe much of the information we receive in school is filtered or tainted, and we are taught to memorize not to question. History is slanted and new concepts or ideas which are outside the accepted position of science are repressed. Organized religion is based on fear, not love. Taking all this into consideration I started to look at the question people had posed to me "Do you think there are outside energy forces that are suppressing your gifts?"

This whole book up until this point has been a record of my life; my childhood awareness of having "purpose"; and my internal awareness that I am a spark of the Divine Light. My thoughts began to congeal and I started to see things from a larger perspective. All the thoughts and ideas I'm expressing in this writing are not new, but I get a sense I am to share them through my eyes.

Time to Be ALIVE

For a long time now I've related to the world as energy; energy that I can see, hear and feel. When I see a person I see a spirit, when I do my healing, I work with energy, when I work with sound I work with vibration and frequencies. It is as if I'm sensing the world around me before I see it. I know and understand that we are one with "God". I realize as a spirit, I live in many dimensions simultaneously, and this planet is just one of the dimensions I'm in. I have this knowing, yet I also live in the reality of earth, and I am subject to its pitfalls. You have witnessed this through reading my story. Even through the pitfalls I am still aware I'm here for a purpose; I am here to touch people, thousands of people. How that will happen? I'm not sure, but this book is something that has been channeled through me to share with others. For some reason you needed to know me intimately before I shared with you my philosophy, and the depth of the gifts and awareness that I bring to this dimension.

So in Book Two, I will talk about the world through the eyes of energy and we will explore ancient wisdom and its merit in today's world, and it will be expressed through my words as I sense the world and intuitively understand it to be.

I am going to give you the dictionary definitions and Wikipedia's explanation of the words: energy, matter, vibration and frequency, as we will be talking about these things in Book Two.

Book Two
Foreword

Dictionary definitions:

Energy: 1. *force of expression or utterance. 2a. potential forces; inherent power; capacity for vigorous action 2b. [often pl] such forces or power, esp. in action [to apply all one's energies] 3. strength or power efficiently exerted 4a. those resources, as coal, gas, wind, nuclear fuel, and sunlight, from which energy in the form of electricity, heat ,etc. can be produced 4b. the available supply of such resources [an energy shortage] 5. Physics the capacity for doing work: abbrev. E see MATTER (sense 2)*

Matter: (Partial definition) 1. *what a thing is made of; constituent substance or material 2. what all (material) things are made of; whatever occupies space and is perceptible to the senses in some way: in modern physics, matter and energy are regarded as equivalents, mutually convertible according to Einstein's formula, $E = mc2$ (i.e., energy equals mass multiplied by the square of velocity of light); in dualistic thinking, matter is regarded as the opposite of mind, spirit, etc.* (this partial definition pertains to the topics we are discussing i.e., energy)

Frequency: 1a. *[Obs.] the condition of being crowded 1b. crowd 2. the fact of occurring often or repeatedly; frequent occurrence 3. the times any action or occurrence is repeated in a given period 4. Math., Statistics 4a. the number of times an event, value, or characteristic occurs in a given period 4b. ratio of the number of trails in which it can occur (in full relative frequency) 5. Physics the number of periodic oscillations, vibrations, or waves per unit of time: usually expressed in hertz: abbrev f.*

Vibration: 1. *the action of vibrating; specif., 1a. movement back and forth, as of a pendulum; oscillation*

1b. rapid rhythmic movement back and forth; quiver
2. vacillation or wavering, as between two choices or opinions *3. [pl.] emotional qualities or supernatural emanations that are sensed or felt by another person or thing 4. Physics 4a. to–and–fro motion or oscillation of an object, as an elastic body or the particles of a fluid, when it is displaced from the rest position or the rest position of equilibrium, as in transmitting sound 4b. a single, complete oscillation.

Wikipedia's explanations:

Energy: (from the *Greek energeia*, meaning "activity, operation", from - energos, meaning "active, working") is a *scalar physical quantity* that is an attribute of objects and systems that is conserved in nature. In physics *textbooks*, energy is often defined as the ability to do *work* or to cause change.

Several different forms of energy exist to explain all known natural phenomena. These forms include (but are not limited to) *kinetic, potential, thermal, gravitational, sound, light, elastic,* and *electromagnetic* energy. Any form of energy can be *transformed* into another form, but the total energy always remains the same. This principle, the *conservation of energy*, was first postulated in the early 19th Century, and applies to any *isolated system*. According to *Noether's theorem*, the conservation of energy is a consequence of the fact that the laws of physics do not change over time.[2]

Although the total energy of a system does not change with time, its value may depending on the *frame of reference*. For example, a seated passenger in a moving airplane has zero kinetic energy relative to the airplane, but non-zero kinetic energy relative to the *Earth*.

Matter: is anything that has both *mass* and *volume* (takes up *space*). A more rigorous definition is used in

Book Two
Foreword

science: **matter** is what atoms and molecules are made of. Matter is commonly said to exist in four *states* (or *phases*): *solid, liquid, gas* and *plasma*; other phases, such as *Bose–Einstein condensates*, also exist. In everyday human environments, matter is closely related to (and in many contexts equivalent to) *mass*.

In the realm of *relativity*, matter can be equated to *energy* via the equation $E = mc^2$. In the realm of *cosmology*, other forms of matter and energy, such as *dark matter* and *dark energy* are invoked to explain the behavior of the *observable universe*.

Frequency is the number of occurrences of a repeating event per unit *time*. It is also referred to as **temporal frequency**. The **period** is the *duration* of one *cycle* in a repeating event, so the period is the *reciprocal* of the frequency.

Vibration refers to mechanical *oscillations* about an equilibrium point. The oscillations may be *periodic* such as the motion of a pendulum or *random* such as the movement of a tire on a gravel road.

Vibration is occasionally "desirable". For example the motion of a *tuning fork*, the *reed* in a *woodwind instrument* or *harmonica*, or the cone of a *loudspeaker* is desirable vibration, necessary for the correct functioning of the various devices.

More often, vibration is undesirable, wasting *energy* and creating unwanted *sound—noise*. For example, the vibrational motions of *engines*, *electric motors*, or any *mechanical device* in operation are typically unwanted. Such vibrations can be caused by *imbalances* in the rotating parts, uneven *friction*, the meshing of *gear* teeth, etc. Careful designs usually minimize unwanted vibrations.

Time to Be ALIVE

The study of sound and vibration are closely related. Sound, or "pressure waves", are generated by vibrating structures (e.g. *vocal cords*); these pressure waves can also induce the vibration of structures (e.g. *ear drum*). Hence, when trying to reduce noise it is often a problem in trying to reduce vibration.

Please note: for your information, I copied the definitions word for word from the dictionary, and I copy and pasted the Wikipedia's explanation from their website.

Book Two

Part 1
My Deeper Truth
Edgar Cayce once said,
"Life...God, in Its essence is vibration."

Chapter 1

In the deepest part of my center I know we all embody an internal knowing, something so deep it just is.
I am continuing to work on my understanding and acceptance of this knowing as well as share it with you.

To begin with, it is also important to realize, as well as remember, that knowingness comes from the heart, which is the true center of our knowing. Often times I feel we intellectualize our deepest knowing because it is easier for us to think it rather than feel it and communicating it is far easier than living it. For many years I studied "The I Ch'ing" and it teaches that when our intellectual knowing truly becomes a matter of the heart, then and only then can we live it. I strongly believe this is one of the opportunities of this planet.

Within that internal deep knowing, each and every one of us has what I call our Cosmic Consciousness; for we are a Spark of the Divine. People seem to always be looking outside of themselves to find their source when the source or God does not live outside of us at all, it lives within us, for we are the source, we are God!

Time to Be ALIVE

Well that was a subtle beginning! How bold can I be? So I guess now is the time to share with you my thoughts regarding who we are intrinsically. Before I begin I'd like to point out that these are my thoughts, they are my truths, and I feel these thoughts are worth sharing, but it is important when reading anything, or listening to lectures that you read or listen with your own discernment.

Chapter 2

I have always imagined being blown into trillions or more sparks and within all those sparks, lives the whole. I imagine we are those sparks; within each of us lives a spark, and the sparks are energy, energy vibrating at different frequencies yet infinitely "one."

Things are shifting on this planet. You can see it in the political and economic challenges of our times. It is time to move out of the manipulated fear based reality we have been living in and into a conscious awakened state of being. It is time to acknowledge we are energy, and to learn how to work with our energy.

This should not be too much of a leap as science has concluded that we are ENERGY.

As I stated earlier my understanding of energy is that it is a vibration. That vibration is our Spark of the Divine, or what one might call "spirit". This vibration connects us to all things so as a result, within each of us exist omnipotence, and in this book it is what I will be referring to as "Cosmic Consciousness" or our "Spark of the Divine". It is a concept that is difficult for most of the human race to wrap their head around, yet intrinsically we know deep within us that we are a "Spark of the Divine". We truly, simply know. It is from this point I choose to go forward with this book. I choose to talk with you about *your power,* your "Cosmic Consciousness". We will also be looking at what blocks that power, or suppresses that power and what that means to us, and suggestions on how you can awaken to your power.

Time to Be ALIVE

We will also be talking about energy, and in the context of energy we will be discussing how sound relates to energy, how sound stimulates you and how certain frequencies can open the portals to your "inner dimensions". As I stated at the beginning of Part I, Edgar Cayce once said, **"Life..God, in its essence is vibration."**

Author's Note: *My prayer is that sharing my thoughts will give you pause to reflect on your life and the world we live in, will inspire you and stimulate you to go inward to move forward, so let's move forward with my thoughts and ideas regarding, life, God, energy and shifting times.*

We all have what I consider a vibrational essence.

For example my vibrational essence is that of a master healer, and this vibrational essence lives within my DNA, my tissues, my cells, my organs and my bones and when I live in that vibrational essence I am living in my "Cosmic Consciousness". I am acknowledging and living in my God/Goddess Self when I do my healing work; be it sound, energy or hands on healing, I am working from my core essence, and when I am working from my core essence I am one with all. I do not need to think, or wonder about what I'm doing, I just know I know. I know that what flows through me is pure, and when I'm working from that state of purity, I am working with the higher self of the people I work with. I know that when I work I am assisting others to clear their blockages and activate their "Cosmic Consciousness". I know that, and there is a freedom in knowing that. Being in my "Cosmic Consciousness" I also know that I bring through frequencies that are not of this world with my sound work, frequencies that can activate others in the awareness of their power. I have no science to prove this, but it is a knowing that lives within me, and when I operate from that knowing I am in my God/Goddess Essence.

Author's Note: *I am beginning to have a sense that I am also writing this book to bring healing through these written words. As an affirmation to myself; I know I am here to support the planet and the beings on this planet to awaken to their vibrational essence so that we can all live more fully in our "Cosmic Consciousness". I know I am a spirit, living a human experience!*

I am not the only being with a vibrational essence; each and every person has a vibrational essence, as well as the ability to have their own strong certainty of "knowing". Now is the time to be fully conscious of your certainty of knowing and your abilities.

I would also like to mention at this time that I feel strongly our vibrational essence can be awakened and realized through sound. Sound plays an important role in our lives and subtly it stimulates the awareness of our chakra centers. For those of you who are not familiar with chakras, chakras are energy points in our body. The most agreed upon number of chakras in our body are seven (yet in my understanding there are more). They are considered sources of energy for our psychic or spiritual power, therefore when one of our chakra points are blocked or weak, it weakens us spiritually as well as emotionally and physically. Our energy points, or chakra's which are directly connected to our vibrational essence, can be stimulated with certain frequencies. These frequencies can then assist us in opening portals to our inner dimensions. This is why so many ancient cultures used

Time to Be ALIVE

chanting in their ceremonies and spiritual practices. So, in my opinion sound is very important to mankind, and I feel it will play a major part in the healing of our planet as well as the human race. Since we live in a planet of duality there also are certain frequencies that can disrupt your harmonic balance. There are frequencies that can knock you out of your center; disrupt your intrinsic awareness that you are a "Spark of the Divine". There are "other" energy forces that can be utilizing these frequencies to disrupt your power.

Having said this I again choose to remind you that you are a "spark of the divine" and because of that it is absolutely possible for every person to have their own certainty of knowing, to live within the NOW, and be in your "Cosmic Consciousness". It is within your power to live within your light. So, let's explore further.

Chapter 3

It is important for this planet and for the survival of the world as we know it, for all people to put their efforts into remembering who we are. It is important that who and what we are be recognized and embraced by all of us. It is my understanding that this is how we will change the world, support the planet and evolve. I feel deep within myself that the majority of people on this planet also desire this. Another desire of the human race is the quest to understand where we come from and who we are, so now is the perfect time to remember.

I have always sensed that this planet is an interesting experiment in the grander scheme of things. I believe time will tell if this "sense" is accurate or not. I also feel that our internal knowing is shrouded with a veil or cloak of some kind, and oft times our wonder and the magnitude of our Cosmic Consciousness can be forgotten or lost to us for just a moment in cosmic time, which could be a lifetime on earth.

I intimated earlier that most of us have some kind of deep intrinsic awareness of our internal knowing. Often times that deep awareness translates to an intellectual consciousness or thought. This might be where we are getting stuck. If the awareness is living in the mind and not in the heart how can you feel it, live it and be it? Most people still search for it outside themselves, even when they have an inkling of understanding that it lives within. My sense is that it is just too simple and perhaps too scary to look for the concept of divinity within.

Even though I feel a lot of "energy" has been used to suppress our Cosmic Consciousness as well as our power

Time to Be ALIVE

I still observe it is the ultimate quest of most individuals to understand who we are, and where we come from.

The fact that it remains a quest is interesting to me, for I believe that this planet is about remembering what has always been deep inside of us. It leaves me to wonder if this quest has been turned against us or hidden from us by "other" energy forces. Perhaps we have had a cloud around us which has been used to keep us from the truth rather than guiding us to the truth. Perhaps the question posed to me, "could there be other forces working against you" had more merit than I would like to admit. But now it is a question I would like very much to explore with you. Should this planet be more spiritually advanced? Is the density of this planet the only issue we have in exploring and realizing our divinity?

I will acknowledge that one of the challenges or opportunities of this planet deals with the density that exists here, but has this density been complicated by "other" energy forces? Has this "outside" influence of the "other" energy forces left the spirit waiting to be remembered by millions if not billions of people living today? Do these "other" energy forces find it more advantageous to their own agenda to diffuse our intrinsic power by encouraging our confusion and thereby blocking us from fully realizing our Cosmic Consciousness as well as utilizing it? Has our divine right been tampered with?

Book Two
Part 1

Chapter 4

Let's go back to our Cosmic Consciousness. Each and every being or energy has a frequency within their core. Once that frequency is recognized consciously the magic happens. Once it becomes stimulated or activated, it comes alive; filling us with passion, creativity, well being, a sense of wholeness, and a feeling of oneness and with that feeling comes an inner understanding of our own empowerment. When that frequency is stimulated or activated for even a second we can feel a hint of our true essential self. When it is activated over a period of time, we begin to live in that frequency for longer and longer periods and our energy becomes even stronger. As our energy becomes stronger we begin to live in our power and who and what we are can be actualized.

Actually that is how we vibrate infinitely, or as a friend of mine David Weber who lectures and channels the "Rishes" puts it, "When we are in our "flow" the "God/Goddess" consciousness is always flowing through us."

Yes it is possible for us to recognize that the "Cosmic Consciousness" flows through our bodies, but first we must **understand** that the "Cosmic Consciousness" is already flowing through us, has always been flowing through us, and will continue to flow through us, we just need to open ourselves to the concept and finally realize it. With the density of this planet, and the presence of "other energy" forces, our clarity can easily get clouded or as David puts it "blocked". So again, as we can never be reminded of this too many times; whether we recognize it or not "God/Goddess" consciousness is always living or flowing through us. Once we recognize it we can utilize it.

Time to Be ALIVE

What is blocking us? Why do we remain blocked? How can we change this? I will share with you my thoughts regarding this, but before I continue I would like to say a few things about the earth's changes. One of the reasons I feel we have not "flowed" so easily in the past is due to the density of this planet. As many of you know, and for those of you who do not know, earth is in its own major transition. Part of that transition is that the density of the planet is changing, so the density of earth will soon be a non issue for us as it relates to our Cosmic Consciousness. It is from this point I would like to move forward.

So again, what is blocking us? Imagine an energy force with counter intentions towards our natural flow or cosmic frequency as being the culprit. Imagine an "intentional" vibration targeted to unsettle the intrinsic frequency of the masses, thereby blocking the natural flow of mankind. Imagine that these vibrations are being used by a group of energies who have already realized their power, their "magic", their "flow" and with their intentions have created a band of energy or vibration that surrounds this planet. Now imagine the intention of that band of energy is to suppress, or sedate the Cosmic Consciousness of humanity and the stimulus for that energy is fear. Again, the stimulus for that energy is "FEAR".

I strongly feel such suppression exists, and I believe it has created great confusion and havoc for mankind.

At this point I choose to again remind you that you ARE a "Spark of the Divine", and intrinsically you have awareness and knowledge of this fact, and deep within, you have the power to shield yourself from any outside frequencies that are not in your highest and best interest. We ARE powerful beings we just need to remember "our" magic.

So why are so many people still asleep or disconnected or unaware? WHY, I ask myself? I understand hesitation, I understand feeling vulnerable and unsure, but just to stay unaware is difficult for me to wrap my mind around. I also feel there has been a movement on this planet since before the time of Christ to awaken us to our "higher" self, and fight against the "other" energy forces. I feel there have been civilizations who where aware of their "Cosmic Consciousness" who have walked the earth and left there vibration in the land for us to find and utilize for our own awakening process. So again I ask, why are so many still asleep?

Also, because this planet is shifting and with that shifting the density is being dissipated, we no longer have the density of this planet as an excuse. The clouds created by the density are beginning to lift for us, and our "Spark of the Divine", our "Cosmic Consciousness" can be more easily realized at this time. So why are so many people still asleep?

As I see it the only thing that stands between us living in our true Divine Consciousness is our fears and those "other" energy forces know this and understand it, so in a remote way began the illusion of fear long ago. This illusion of fear was needed because these "other" energy forces created an energetic barrier around us, and needed something to activate that barrier. The illusion of fear was the perfect answer. As long as this energetic barrier remains strong, and we continue to respond to the manipulation of fear, they can continue to sedate us and control us all the while keeping mankind repressed. People are repressed and manipulated with such things as religion, (in my opinion this was the first major manipulation archetype), then the educational system. Now there is television, newspapers, media and a multitude of other distractions including survival that continue to take us away from our power. All of these things are being used to control our thoughts and our self image; all in an attempt to keep us from the power that lives within. A lot of time and energy has gone into this plan. It is a major endeavor to keep us "asleep". Why, I ask? What will happen if we wake up?

Again I remind you, if my instincts are correct, fear is the stimulus that activates our sedation, so fear is what we need to eliminate, and the way to eliminate fear is to know that we are a "Spark of the Divine". Once we recognize that we can move into our magic. We can wake up and we can move into our power.

For centuries now the "other" energy forces have been using fear—that natural instinct within us. What we now call fear in the past was nature's yellow caution light. What is now known as fear was an instinct for our self–preservation. Does anyone else see the irony of this? Our instinct of self preservation was never meant to immobilize us; it was meant to save us. When the "fear" instinct arises in the body, it is meant to give us the opportunity to assess the situation we're in and act accordingly. The keyword here is "act". The "other" energy forces understand our natural "fear" instinct, and they amplified it to the point of immobilizing us. This was done so that they could control us and use the fear towards their own means. Now they torment us with it for their own advantage and to in some way enslave us. They have been building this vibrational frequency that surrounds the planet for hundreds of years now. I believe their ultimate intention is to gain power over all mankind and if we do not do something about this, they may just be able to accomplish their goals. We are seeing the outcome of their manipulation and fear tactics in the events that are now occurring in the worldwide political and economic climate.

Now let's imagine what would happen if we were free, and we no longer responded to the fear? What would happen if we were able to discern when we are being cautioned by our instincts or manipulated by induced fear? What would happen if we paid attention and acted from our place of strength and wisdom? What would happen if we took back our control? What if we decided to live in our true power?

It is my instinct that in the beginning the "other" energy force's vibration did not have the same power, as it appears to have now. As an example, imagine a snowball rolling down a mountain and with each turn that little snowball gains momentum, power and strength. With each turn it seems to be getting bigger and closer; shutting out all the light, and as it gets bigger we seem to get smaller. Yet in the darkest hour, when all seems lost, Divine Consciousness, or our power within has the ability to come alive and destroy the snowball, destroy the power of those outside forces.

Think of Cosmic Consciousness as a charge of dynamite, once detonated it can blow the gigantic snowball apart, not to mention the fears. We just need to make the choice. Do we live in our power or do we stay asleep?

Author's Note: *As I am writing this, I have no idea what examples will come up because basically the "Cosmic Consciousness" is flowing through me as I write. Presently I'm writing about "other" energy forces, frequencies and vibrations. When you think of vibration does the word "sound" enter your mind? Sound actualizes energy being vibrated. Sound is vibration that you can hear and sometimes feel. Just now I used a random example, that perhaps might not be so random after all, because within the word detonate lives the word "tone". I could not have planned a better example if I tried. I know sound can destroy, as well as create. I feel this is a subtle yet perfect example of divine intervention or our Cosmic Consciousness at work. By utilizing a random thought or random circumstance it brings us back to the whole. How cool is this? What a wonderful reminder this has been for me. This is what I would call an example of living life in your "flow" as my dear friend David would say. Being "in your flow" is a message I feel many teachers and healers are now ministering to the world. So what is the importance of flow in relationship to what I was talking about? Even thought I haven't come to the end of my thoughts, I would venture to guess it has everything to do with what I am ultimately writing about. So without apparent knowing, yet with ultimate knowing, I used an analogy that not only encapsulates the word "tone" but gives an example of breaking apart something that is blocking the light. I invite you to imagine if you will, every moment infused with your divine awareness, your Cosmic Consciousness supporting you in your life's "flow". Imagine yourself walking in your light, imagine the darkness fading. Imagine "you" in your*

Book Two
Part 1

Cosmic Consciousness. I ask you, is that not an amazing picture?

Its hard to remember that when I sat down to write this I thought I was going to jot down a few thoughts that would convey my deeper inner wisdom, but as the words continue to pour from me I realize that this was becoming a book not just a few paragraphs. I realize that what I am attempting to share with anyone who might read this is the simple expression of "my" truth. Yet on this planet is there such a thing as simple? The truth is simple but that simplicity is woven into a mass of complexity, and once we break away from the complexity we will be left with the simple truth.

Time to Be ALIVE

Book Two

Part II
Random Thoughts Coming Together

Chapter 1

There have been moments, and when I say moments I speak of them in Cosmic Time, for on this planet these cosmic moments can literally be days, weeks, months and at times even years. So again, there have been cosmic moments when I have experienced the density of this planet as if it were quicksand, and the more I resisted the further and faster I sank into the mire, yet when I stopped resisting and took a breath and just surrendered I was always released from that "sinking" phenomenon. The earlier "dark night of the soul" experience is a major example of what I'm attempting to describe. It wasn't until I just surrendered that things could change.

So what changed; the circumstances or my attitude?

At times both, but in all cases my attitude needed to shift. In all my life experiences' it is always at the point of surrender that my "Cosmic Consciousness" takes over and leads the way through whatever darkness or mire, or illusion I am experiencing at the time. As I write this, I am acutely reminded that during each and every one of those moments, surrender and breath would have changed the "energy", could have changed the course of the experience. By just having the ability to remember to just be still and breathe, to move back into my center, to focus my intention. This is the power of our "Cosmic Consciousness". Too often we simply get stuck in the mire.

Time to Be ALIVE

So what is surrender? For many the word surrender brings up a lot of issues. Does surrender conjure up the idea of giving up, becoming a limp rag and letting people walk all over you? The literal definition of surrender is "yielding or giving up something in favor of something else", so is surrender the appropriate word? Is surrender the proper word for letting go of our ego self so we can be more fully present with our higher self? Is surrender the appropriate word for letting go of the beliefs and ideas that have been imposed on us that have no relevance to our true essence in favor of living in our own truth?

We often operate in a mode of automatic pilot. We are often reacting to life rather than creating our life. From the time we are born we are being manipulated. We are not really encouraged to have our own thoughts or have our own power. As I write this I realize how it confirms my concept that we are being suppressed. I also realize that when I speak of surrender, I am actually surrendering the false beliefs that have either been imposed on me or I have adopted out of insecurity or low self esteem in favor of my deeper "inner" truth. So when I speak of surrender, it is not because I'm giving up, no, not at all, instead I am choosing myself over false concepts. Perhaps that is why "surrender" seems to be a recurring theme in my life.

Book Two
Part II

Chapter 2

I realize that when I write about this I make it seem simple, and in truth it is basically simple. So again we come back to that concept of simple. Can it be simple?

I realize I am a spirit experiencing this human experience as we all are. I know, as I am sure we all do how difficult surrender **(based on my understanding of surrender)** can seem to be, especially here in this dimension. I understand that when life is at its most difficult it does not appear to be easy or simple. In fact if I had one word to describe it, the word I'd use would be "overwhelming". More than anything I understand how challenging it actually seems to be to be able to stop and remember who we intrinsically are. It may be difficult and challenging, but it is necessary that we begin to do this. Everyday we must summon the courage that lives within us to be all that we can be and all that we are. There are often times when this requires supreme effort, but we are supreme beings; we are the "Spark of the Divine", so this ability lives and breaths within us all, we just need to remember and surrender to our higher self. This "simple" truth is necessary for us to remember now.

Remembering who we are is so important to all of us, especially now for it feels as if this planet is in a "dark night of the soul" experience itself. I know that if the masses do not choose to take a stand and call back our power we are all at risk of getting caught in the quicksand of this shift over and over again. For this purely selfish reason I would encourage everyone to remember their power. It truly is simple, we just need to remember. I would also like to remind you on a grander level, we are all one and any indiscretion or misfortune happening to one is happening to us all. So for the sake of ourselves and the sake of humanity my vote is that we wake up and remember who we are.

I absolutely know that what I am committing to paper is not new knowledge. I know this with every fiber of my being, for it is knowledge as old as time itself, or our understanding of time on this planet. It is wisdom that each and every living vibration understands and knows intrinsically. I am basically just writing it in my words, and as I do this I become more fully engaged in my own power.

Book Two
Part II

The following are pictures and examples of various subjects, which have been or will be discussed in this book.

This is an image of the "*Tree of Life*" within the "*Flower of Life*", and I've included a description from Wikipedia about the "*Tree of Life*"

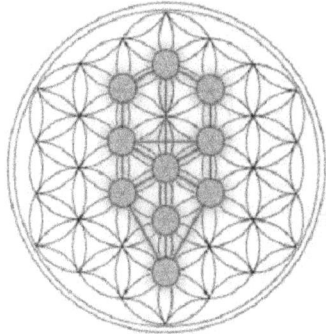

"The concept of a many-branched tree illustrating the idea that all life on earth is related has been used in science, religion, philosophy, mythology and other areas. A **tree of life** is variously, a) a mystical concept alluding to the interconnectedness of all life on our planet, b) a metaphor for common descent in the evolutionary sense, and c) a motif in various world theologies, mythologies and philosophies."

I believe this accurately describes why the lights were formed in this pattern when they appeared to me in Kona. The symbol as expressed above perfectly describes the message I am bringing to you. How better to embody it within me than with this symbol!

Here is another example of the Flower of Life, which I believe to be the most recognized symbol of Sacred Geometry.

The information in Wikipedia is well worth reading, and too long insert here.

This is a picture of the Star of David, which is also known as a six–pointed star.

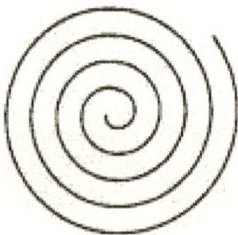

This is a picture of a spiral, a wonderful ancient symbol which I perceive shows us of the continuum of spirit.

Book Two
Part II

These are pictures of my trip to Egypt and the Orb that was captured above my head while toning in the sarcophagus. I know this is when my "ancient" sound was being re-activated. What a wonderful affirmation of my intuition.

Day 7 ~ Initiation Rites in King's Chamber

As you can see the King's Chamber is filled with orbs after the ceremony.

I wanted to share with you some crop circles. These are just two examples. I urge you to go online and visit various crop circle sites to view more of this magnificent earth art, and if you ever have an opportunity to visit a crop circle in person, please do so.

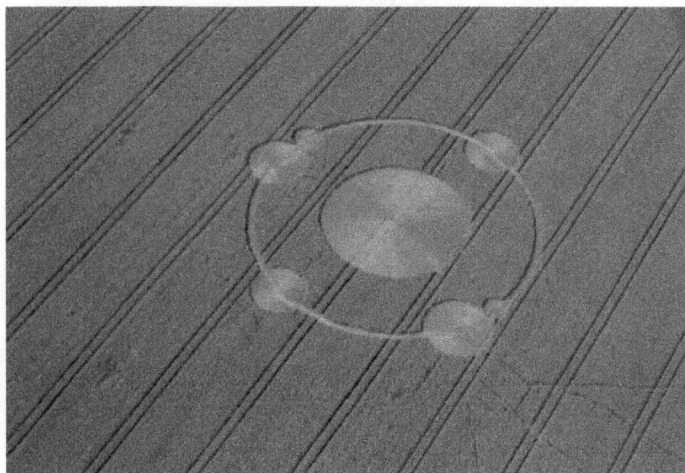

Above are a series of pictures of my sound as evaluated by Dr. Emoto's Lab in Japan. You can see how the sound is breaking up a damaged molecule and reforming it, starting from an embryonic state to a perfect crystalline form. This is a visual example of the power of the ancient sound that comes through me.

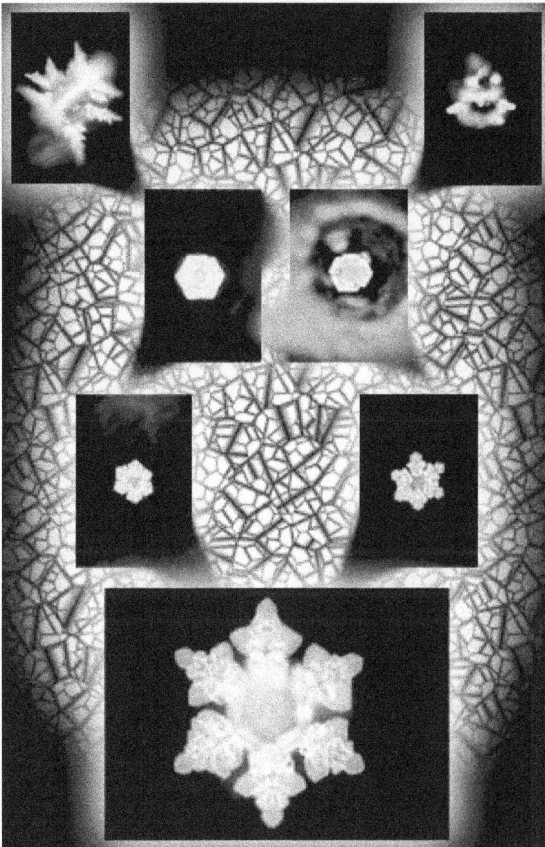

Time to Be ALIVE

I also thought you might enjoy several of the sacred sites my travels have taken me to. There is amazing magic in these locations. I also would like to remind you that there is magic within you.

Machu Picchu, Peru

Giza Plateau, Egypt

Silbury Hill, England

Book Two
Part II

Book Two

Part III
Changing Times

Chapter 1

The times are changing, yet in this dimension change is a constant but right now there is an acceleration going. On. I feel the acceleration, and the shifting especially in my own frequency. I liken this shift to a major growth spurt. In one's lifetime on this planet, we are exposed to subtle shifting day after day, and when suddenly a big growth spurt comes along we are totally amazed and taken off guard. It is somewhat like the momentous growth spurt we experience in our pre to early teens. One day we are 5' 1" and the next day we seem to be 5'6". Even though we know we are going to "grow" it somehow always takes us off guard. The shifts and changes are imminent but they seem to always be a surprise to us as well as the people around us. That is what is happening here on this planet. This is a gigantic shift that is happening now, and it promises to be quite cataclysmic.

We need to remember how unnerving it can be in our personal lives when we are in the process of a major change. The stress that is associated with change. At first it is shocking, but then you settle into the change and accept it and sometimes even marvel at the wonder of it. Like us, earth does not escape this process for change is a part of its daily life as well. Earth's changes are reminiscent of ours; some of them are subtle but some are quite tremendous.

Time to Be ALIVE

Earth has gone through many changes in its past and I believe this mighty planet will be able to handle the changes that are occurring now. So the big question for me is not how earth will handle the changes, but how will we handle the changes taking place? I strongly feel that during this time it is even more important for us to be aware of whom we are intrinsically; important for us to remember our "Cosmic Consciousness". Being aware is going to be a key factor in riding out the wave during this significant shift.

Sometimes I sense without being cognitively aware of it; people are feeling as if they are getting lost in the shift. There has been this undercurrent of energy for a while now that has been affecting our psyche; couple that with the events that are happening on this planet and it has been an uneasy time, "vibrationally" speaking. The shift is actually forcing us to have more cognitive awareness of who we are "intrinsically".

Actually this is a good thing. As the veils are lifting more information is available to us, information that has always been there, and information we have always had access to, but due to the density of this planet it has not always been evident to us.

At the same time we are experiencing the shifting on planet earth the "other" energy forces are continuing to suppress the masses, blocking us from our power. I'd like you to consider what a dilemma the earth changes are creating for the "other" energy forces. As I stated before, I believe that the shifts that are occurring now are making it easier for people to realize their "Cosmic Consciousness", which makes the project of suppressing us even more difficult. Therefore as the density of earth is in flux and is shifting, it seems that the grip of the "other" energy forces is becoming even tighter. I can feel it happening on the cellular level. It seems to be very similar to the power struggle that occurs at times with children and parents. There are times parents feel they have the best interest of their children in mind so sometimes they tend to hold on tighter as the child grows into themselves and begins to explore who they are. I feel when this happens the parents are afraid of letting go, afraid that harm will come to their children, afraid of losing them.

I use the analogy loosely, however, I do believe, in relationship to the "other" energy forces; on some level the need to maintain a position of power originally began with the idea of doing what was best for all mankind, but all too soon it turned into something more sinister and spiritually detrimental. The "other" energy forces may still believe that their way is the best way, but I do feel that the potent exhilaration of having power over something has taken charge of these "other" energy forces and because of this the "true" cosmic powers of these "other" energy forces have gotten lost in their own darkness, by repressing the light in others.

As people we have all experienced having power over someone, as well as an understanding of how to manipulate the truth to serve our purpose. I can give you several examples: the bully on the playground who taunts children either smaller or younger; women who exploit their sexuality; men who dominate women; parents who control their children instead of guiding them. We all understand how it works. We all have done it at one time or another. So we understand that the only way to have that kind of power over something is to instill fear in those you chose to have power over. Once you have established the fear it is simple to manipulate and control, but it is just as important to remember that this control and manipulation works only until the victim begins to realize they also have power.

I have also observed that this behavior pattern of fear and manipulation tends to leave internal scars, for the fear seems to constantly work at undermining its victims and it takes great determination and will to rise above the fear, but we can rise above the fear and we can continue to assert our power over the fear. I believe this behavior archetype started centuries ago, with the "other" energy forces, and it has filtered down into our own behavior patterns today. This behavior archetype serves two purposes: 1. the common acceptance of the practice of manipulation and control. 2. it has given the "other" energy forces the ability to continue on a subversive level to repress the power that lives and breathes within us.

By continually instilling fear, they control and manipulate, and when they see the masses attempting to break away, they create another situation that will hold the masses in tow, and thus the cycle continues around and around, and around.

Just the thought of it takes my breath away. This very thought or concept is hypnotic; taking me out of my power and moving me back into darkness and fear. I am experiencing it now in just writing about it. Can you see how simple it is to be driven off-course? There are societal patterns and behavior archetypes that have evolved over hundreds of years that to this day continue to have influence over us.

Book Two
Part III

Author's Note: Caroline Myss has lectured, and written about various archetypes that are acculturated within us. I suggest you explore some of her work. It has been years since I attended her workshops but I found her work relevant and laced with humor. Something we all need during these trying times.

Are these patterns being used to stifle the intrinsic power of the masses? I believe they are, and the only way to break the patterns will be to be conscious of when they are occurring. Once conscious we can shift the reality of the situation. We can breathe and change our point of view. When we learn to recognize the manipulation it will be easier to shift it. I also feel that the more enlightened the masses become there will be less manipulation to shift.

Book Two
Part III

Chapter 2

In my observation, there seems to be a complacence or ambivalence among the masses. It seems as if the fear that has evolved over the centuries has placed a fog around us. Are we so busy attempting to maintain some kind of status quo in our lives that we do not even question the world around us? Has this been manipulated by design or are we truly complacent? It is so sad to see this happening. How long has it been since we questioned what is happening? Have we ever had permission to question? If we had permission would we question? How many things in this world make sense? How often do you stop and questions the inconsistency of the world you live in? Have we become ambivalent? Are we content to just "exist"? Is this the reason we are here?

Instead of waking up to our power, instead of living in our power, it seems as if we've become complacent and have misplaced our will to discover ourselves. Oh yes we exist, but is existing truly living? Is status quo really the best path? I feel that continued ambivalence on the part of the masses will somehow shift or have an impact on the evolution that is occurring. How that impact will affect us is unclear at the moment, but I feel as if there will be needless repercussions if we do not wake up.

Whether we wake up or not, I know the evolution will happen but I am inclined to reiterate again; my intuition suggests there are consequences that will occur should blatant disregard continue once people are aware and can consciously choose. I also know that it is not too late. It is important for us, all of us, to pay attention. It is one thing to be asleep for a while, but to consistently close our eyes even when the light is attempting to come in; that is another story. I would like to say: WAKE UP! It is definitely time to WAKE UP!

Since earth is experiencing its' own transition, and earth is becoming less dense, I strongly suspect or perhaps a better word would be that I "feel" the "other" energy forces have been re-enforcing the vibrational field that surrounds this planet, because as I stated earlier I do *feel* it. As I already mentioned they are tightening their grip. These vibrational fields serve to keep us asleep, which is exactly what the "other" energy forces want, and if we choose to stay asleep they will get their way. If we awoke it would put a damper on, if not destroy to a great extent the "other" energy forces' power over us! What would the world be like then? What would the world be like, I wonder? Are we ready to be responsible? Are we ready to truly be in charge of our destiny? Sometimes I feel that in looking at the overall situation it may seem bleak, but we do have options, we do have a choice and we can exercise our choice at anytime. What are you ready for?

I am not what one would consider a sterling example of an en**light**ened being, but I do know my intention is to live more fully in my vibrational essences each and everyday. So from my perspective I am certain that if every being were to have an intention of living in their full vibrational essence every day, our world would change in a very positive way. For me this is a simple truth.

Chapter 3

I know in taking our power back waking up is the first step, but it is imperative that once awake every being recognize the power they have within themselves. Awaking and recognizing our power is crucial to our survival of free will and freedom on this planet! Once we recognized our power, we need to be responsible with our power.

I understand because of the acculturation that has been imposed on us for centuries, this might seem to be a difficult process for many, but even though it may be a difficult process to recognize and own the power that lives within us, it is certainly not impossible. In my point of view this must become our greatest quest; to find our power within. Once we can recognize our power the possibilities that are open to us are endless! Again, the possibilities open to us are endless!! Take a moment to breathe this in and absorb it.

Let me remind you again that you are a Spark of the Divine, and within you your "Cosmic Consciousness" exists. This is so important for us to remember and focus on; which is why I keep repeating it throughout the book.

Once again after the first step of awakening, we need to acknowledge that we are an aspect of the divine spirit, then we must realize and understand how important it is to break away from the centuries of imposed suppression. Breaking away will be a significant factor in the future of this planet, a very significant factor. How we choose to reconstruct the world will also be critical as well. When we do make the choice to take our power back, we will be rebuilding the world. I repeat, when we do make the choice to take our power back, we will be rebuilding the world. This is an important as well as sobering thought. How will we rebuild the world? Will it be built with love and acceptance or will we fall back into the patterns we are attempting to escape? Choosing the kind of world we would like, and creating it is a major responsibility. A challenge I believe we are ready for, and one that we can manifest, yet it is important that we fully realize the magnitude of the choices that are upon us.

Book Two

Part IV
Memories of the Beginning

Chapter 1

Often I have wondered how this all began. If we are all a spark of the divine how could the "other" energy forces get to a point of having power over others? If all things are one, and all things are equal, then how could this take place and why do we have any issues at all? I am also willing to ask myself if this is an issue to anyone else or just with myself. So you see I really have given this a great deal of thought.

I admit I have a memory of this planet having a slightly different reality than it does now. It was a faint memory that has gotten stronger over time. I remember beings of a higher consciousness on this planet; they were beings of light who understood their power, but the longer they stayed on this planet the denser their vibration became. Because of this many left before they would become too dense to leave, but there were some who did not leave in time or chose to stay. It is my understanding they originally came here on a discovery mission, to understand earth's frequencies and possibilities. Because the vibrations of the beings that remained here became denser the strength of their abilities began to fade. Before their abilities began to fade, they had conscious access to all the dimensions and were able to travel and communicate telepathically without effort. In the end, the beings gravitated towards the vortices if they were not already near them because they were able to retain some of their memories as well as powers in these locations.

Sound played an important role in the early development of earth, and continues to play an important role in our development today. Frequencies and harmonics were and are used to create. Not only were they used to create they have been used to record the wisdom of the ancient ones for every person to have access to. That information is recorded and lives in the structures of the ancient sites today.

Could this be the reason so many people, when opening to their awareness of their powers seek these sites to visit?

Author's Note: *I just reread this and loosely translated it resembles some of the "traditional" creation story. Up until this time I had never recognized the similarities. I guess there is a morsel of universal truth in all things.*

Book Two
Part IV

Chapter 2

Now for a moment let's move more deeply into my perceptions. Just imagine that this whole universe was created by the Divine All, of which we are a spark. Would this mean that we participated in the creation? Did we have a hand in this madness we call Earth? I believe we did participate in the creation of this planet, and decided to utilize its density. I feel the beings who explored this planet realized it could be utilized in a specific way and from that point the plans were set in motion. They understood that their source of light diminished the longer they remained here. Now again, just imagine, because of its density this universe was to became a game, a game to experience who and what we are, kind of like hide and seek. This planet was perfect for this, not only was their density on earth there was also duality, light and dark, creating another dimension to the density; an experiential dimension. So the plan was put in motion. Hide the spirit so we can seek it; a wonderful experiential game. There was another consequence of this planet; once here there came to be a sense of separation, which in turn spawned a deep sense of longing. Somehow this sense of longing provided another twist to the game.

So the whole reason the game was established was because of the density of this planet which made it easy for the spirit to get lost. The aspect of the separation along with the duality enhanced the experiential opportunities. Now, imagine the game was set up to create blocks and diversions to not only challenge our spirit but ultimately engage our spirit, so that the spirit could be realized. This planet was the perfect atmosphere for such a challenge. In my mind, its like spirit was bored within the nothingness of the all, and decided to create a diversion, and "the game" was the outcome and this planet the perfect atmosphere.

Now for a moment, imagine that within the parameters of any game there are those who grasp the game quicker than others, and because of this they become experts in the game. At that point the game becomes open to the possibility of cheating. When this happens, as I believe it did, it was an opportunity for the "experts" to gain unfair advantage over the other participants. Perhaps these energy forces found the vortices? Perhaps they joined forces with the ancient ones? Perhaps everything that is unfolding is part of a divine plan or the "game"? Perhaps there is more than one conclusion? Since we are speculating, let's continue with my imagination.

Imagine the "Divine All" setting up the circumstances for excitement and experience as well as remembering. Does this sound like planet earth? After all, this planet is filled with diversity and experiences. This is a universe of duality as well as a density. It is capable of hiding the "spark" of light that IS within all things. Within the context of that awareness lays the game; hide and seek.

Now comes the interesting part. Imagine a group of energies very skilled at the game who begin to cheat, and while cheating, they engage in suppressing the masses so that the masses are constantly being blocked in completing the objective of the game; to remember. I believe this is the scenario in which we became engulfed. I also feel that over the myriad of years, somewhere along the way, the game got lost. Now, there is total confusion over what the game is, the objective of the game and why the game was even started in the first place. In the confusion it seems as if we have forgotten how to remember. I question is that part of the plan? Is this the outcome of "free will"? Is this just laziness? Whatever the scenario is, I strongly feel it is time to remember!

It is not that the "other" energies have more power than you or I, because we are all capable of magic, but as I stated before perhaps things got confused. In the context of the game have the "other" energy forces forgotten its purpose? Has their enjoyment of having power over others become more gratifying than participating in a collaboration of power? Has our awareness and the concept of oneness been lost within an agenda of corrupted power? Could this be one of the hazards of duality and a sense of separation?

Book Two
Part IV

Chapter 3

There is a great deal of convolution and confusion that has occurred through the ages, because not only did the game seem to get lost, we seem to have gotten off track ourselves by being complacent. Granted we have had encouragement to remain complacent, but none the less we have become complacent. Yet I know the spirit is infinite and is just waiting within us to be remembered. Since things are changing and the density of this planet is shifting, the veils are becoming thinner, so connecting with ourselves can be easier than ever before, it is just a matter of letting ourselves be open to the possibility.

Having said all of this, it seems that those energies we have spoken about and the acculturation of centuries of suppression or manipulation needs to be recognized and we need to deal with that as well. We fully need to realize the archetypes that have been developed on this planet over time. The misconceived concepts and beliefs that have been spawned over the centuries on this planet that seem to have power over us can now be recognized, and once recognized can be diminished. They are, for a lack of a better word an illusion which needs to be broken apart for us to fully remember our power, our intrinsic power; for we are a "Spark" of the Divine, a wonderful and glorious Cosmic Consciousness waiting to be realized.

Chapter 4

I keep sensing I need to introduce another analogy at this point for clarity, so I will. Imagine, if you will, a new born child, truly filled with wonder and filled with light, not to mention access to other dimensional realities as well as to their own divine consciousness. As time passes the density of this planet, as well as dealing with a physical body begins to wear on the child and its wonder and access to other dimensions begins to erode. With this in mind, it is easy to see how our divine spark, our divine consciousness gets clouded and more recessed as our time on this planet goes on.

Now image the energy of hundreds and hundreds of years of fear, suppression, uncertainty, helplessness, and something that feels like true isolation mixed in with confusion swirling around you. No longer are you a spark of light; free, weightless and conscious, but you are a spark of light buried in darkness and it is becoming more and more difficult to realize your light, and your consciousness is fading slowly then faster and faster, until over time; and in earth time that is maybe two years for most beings, it becomes a faint memory, still present, but so buried its difficult to remember. Now it seems that all there is surrounding you are voices; voices telling you how to be, how to feel, how to think, how to believe, as well as do this or do that. Oh it's so overwhelming just to write about. Is it any wonder we become numb? What a solution, but being numb takes you out of the confusion of this planet.

Author's Note: *As I was writing this passage, I suddenly woke up and there were 4 pages of typed ks on the page. I am experiencing this on such a deep level that I actually numbed out and left my body for a while, at least 4 pages worth of ks. This brought home to me the impact of what I am writing.*

Is there any wonder why addiction is so prevalent? Could the need to remain numb have something to do with it?

How Are We Going To Stop This? It is a very simple answer. It is an answer that lives within each of us. It is simple yet only within the circle of life does it get convoluted.

Book Two
Part IV

Book Three

Foreword

So What Is The Answer?

We have discussed my imagination of how it all began, yet as we know this is only my contention and it may or may not resonate as truth for you, but there is something that I believe we can agree upon; things are in a state of serious flux on this planet. How are we going to deal with this? My response would be; recognize you're Power! Recognize your power and begin to use that power to counter the vibrations being hurled at you from those "other" energy forces who over time have become more interested in having power over us, rather than supporting us in the exploration of our power within. I continue to remind you that even with the density of this planet combined with centuries of acculturation to suppress our intrinsic power, it is still available to us, we just need to wake up and recognize who we truly are. It has been hidden but once we seek we shall find. Once we do that it is incumbent for us to fully recognize the magnitude of this power and learn how to hone our power in a positive way, for every being has the choice on this planet as to how they will "be" in their power once it is recognized, and the choice of how to use it. What will your choice be?

So my prayer is that once we recognize our intrinsic power, we will make the choice to use it wisely. If enough of us do this, and our intention is pure, we will negate the frequencies that are being used to repress us, and we can choose to use our power to encourage others to fully explore the wonder of their own power. When this happens, the world will be a different place. The choice truly belongs to us, which path will you choose?

Author's Note: *Ideas and thoughts are rushing through me at such a tremendous pace. For sometime now I have remembered myself in other dimensions where I can telepath my thoughts, so sometimes I feel very limited by the tools we use on this planet to communicate with. Sometimes I wonder if I will remember everything or adequately express all the thoughts rushing through me. I guess I need to leave that wonder to my divine consciousness, and trust that all that need be written will be written. Again I need to surrender!*

Book Three

Part I
How To Awaken

Chapter 1

What are some of the ways to activate your intrinsic power, your Cosmic Consciousness?

One of the simplest ways, and one of the oldest and perhaps most enduring ways to communicate was with symbols. This was the way the ancient ones used to communicate on this planet. So can symbols open us, and activate us? Symbols in their purest intentional form could be used to remember your Cosmic Consciousness. Having said this, we must consider that over time the meaning of symbols have been convoluted and can often be more confusing than defining.

As an example, take the symbol of the spiral. Was it telling us we are infinite; or is it describing the process of life; or is it a warning about how easy we can get lost in the spiral of life? There is logic to all of these, and I imagine depending on the stage of consciousness you are in, each would be relevant.

Also symbols have been used by various organizations because of their power and meaning, but they have been used with very different emphasis on their meaning. Take the six pointed star as an example. It is a powerful symbol with incredible meaning and magic, and because of that it has been adopted by Judaism as the Star of David, and is also one of the symbols of Satanism or devil worship. There is an interesting book, *"The Six Pointed Star"*, by O.J. Graham which presents this point with more detail and clarity.

The point I am attempting to make is simple; symbols have power, and their power can be construed or interpreted to express different ideologies, and these ideologies often seem to be juxtapose yet the basic symbol remains the same. As I mentioned earlier, these ancient symbols carry magic within them, and that magic can be directed in different ways.

Author's Note: *Please remember my earlier story about my fascination with the astrology magazines that were filled with glyphs or symbols. What were those symbols triggering in me?*

I believe symbols were initially meant to assist us in our remembrance, and trigger our memory, which I feel they can still do when they are in a pure state. An example of this is the phenomenon of the crop circles that seem to magically appear in fields of crops across the world and have for centuries. However this phenomenon has seemed to expand and blossom over the last 20 years, and the center of the activity seems to be in England. This I consider to be **cosmically relative** due to the state of flux earth is experiencing. Even though there is great controversy surrounding the crop circles as to where they come from as well as their authenticity I feel they are powerful. It is what I call earth art with symbols that are given without instruction, leaving us to our own devices and imagination; therefore I believe they can be utilized to activate our memory.

Book Three
Part I

Author's Note: *There are many wonderful websites devoted to the crop circles and most of them have pictures which I believe are worth a thousand words. I suggest you look up these websites, and without reading, look at the pictures. Feel what the symbols within the pictures are telling you. You might be surprised by what they reveal. While you are looking at the pictures, listen to a CD, and I would suggest considering listening to one of mine. The sound coupled with the images might prove very interesting in your awakening.*

However, outside of the crop circles I believe that most symbols of magic and light have also been used to confuse and mislead us. They have been misused for selfish endeavors, and over time their purity and magic has been tarnished, making it more difficult for us to fully comprehend their original intent.

I would be remiss if I did not mention sacred geometry while we are on the subject of symbols, as the study of sacred geometry lives in symbols. ***"Sacred Geometry is an ancient art and science which reveals the nature of our relationship to the cosmos. Its study unfolds the principle of oneness."*** I intuitively understand sacred geometry and the role it plays in our "Cosmic Consciousness". It relates to our connectedness, and in the study of sacred geometry live symbols; and symbols are one of the tools to activate the memory of our oneness. Although I do possess the intuitive ability to grasp the concept of sacred geometry, I do not possess the intellectual prowess to go much beyond what I've already written, because sacred geometry is a science, and science is not my forté. So if this has captured your attention, I would suggest you utilize the Web as a resource to find more detailed information. It is a fascinating study and there are many learned scholars who have written articles and books on the subject. There are far too many good ones for me to single one out.

Chapter 2

Some people might consider prayer to be a way to re-activate our intrinsic power, but for me it doesn't resonate as a true path to self realization, but more like a resource for support and comfort. It seems to me that prayer is a way to confirm our self realization, and acts more as a directive for our power than an activation of our power. I am in no way denouncing prayer as a positive form of expression. I'm just not resonating with it as being the best tool to "activate" our power. I do believe in the power of prayer and the power of our thoughts, as they are both masterful ways to manifest. I just feel like we need to understand and awaken the power within us cognitively to be most effective when using prayer. Once we have done that, and we are working from our "Cosmic Consciousness" we will have greater access through prayer to our amazing ability to manifest and create.

Time to Be ALIVE

Chapter 3

What about religion? Religion is a slippery subject. It is a delicate subject, one with many nuances and points of view. To me it opens up a barrel of worms, and should probably have a whole book devoted to its corruption and manipulation, which has all been done in the name of God. Am I being too bold? If this is offending you, I suggest you just skip over my thoughts about religion, as I am afraid you will be absolutely aghast by the rest of what I feel. I see religion as a way to separate people from people and more importantly from their power, rather than truly connecting us to our oneness, our wholeness, as well as our true power. Religion drives a wedge between our "self" and God. After all, if you really look at religion, most of its teachings are fear based, not love based. For centuries religion or the forces behind religion have taken fragments of truth, coupled with the knowing that people on this planet desire to realize their connection to something greater than what they understand themselves to be, and have used it against us. From a simple piece of truth, a morsel of knowledge, it has been relatively easy for them to create an elaborate manipulation which has been used to repress the human spirit rather than activate it.

At this point again, I want to sincerely tell you that I do not feel that all religious people are corrupt, just the opposite. Most of these individuals are seeking to find their connection, and in that innocence they have been hoodwinked. It is the organization of religion that I take issue with, and what the religious organizations teach their followers.

Time to Be ALIVE

I understand how challenging it is for most people to wrap their minds around this information, especially with all our acculturation. So how can a manipulation of this magnitude be possible? How could thousands of people, that soon became millions of people have been so utterly brainwashed? How? You might ask.

It is really quite simple. Take the fact that we have entered into this world with a conscious spirit that within approximately two years gets buried in the density of this dimension; but even though our conscious awareness is faint, we still resonate with what I will call universal truth. These "other" energy forces, who I have mentioned before, have their own personal agenda regarding people's recognition of "a universal truth". They realized that they could use morsels of this universal truth, to entice the masses. In turn the masses would resonate with it and thus be drawn towards those morsels of truth in their attempt to make a connection with something greater. Once they suck you in, the "fun" can begin.

So organized "faith" was born and the bed of manipulation as well as misinformation became ripe with followers, and the lure is those fragments of universal truth that all organized religions are based on. I see time and again that in religion the whole concept of the universal truth gets lost to us over and over again in the ever alluring cesspool of power and greed. Even when those fragments of truth are recognized by the seekers and there appears to be light to illuminate the darkness, again the real truth gets repressed through some form of fear based manipulation. Once our hopes are opened we get led down what I feel, is an even darker path, a path that attempts to keep us from knowing the "full truth" of who and what we are within. We've been snared in a trap

Book Three
Part I

that is meant to lead us away from our "Spark of the Divine", and for centuries it has worked. From where I stand it appears they have honed their "craft" into a nearly perfect art form. I point out "nearly perfect", for there is still time to awaken.

Since I was a child I have not trusted religion. It always felt like they were asking me to look for something outside myself, yet I have always had this knowing that spirit lived within me. Religion did not seem to support this awareness. When I was about 8 years old I was in Sunday school. My parents were Baptist, so that was the religion I was raised in. One Sunday our Sunday school teacher told us that we should not have Catholic friends. Well, I was aghast, I simply could not believe my ears. Being the person that I am, I challenged this. I said, "But I thought we are suppose to love everyone, isn't that what the Bible says?" My poor Sunday school teacher made every attempt she could to explain, but she just could not convince me that I should not be friends with Catholics. This was not something I could give into without something plausible to support that teaching. It went against every fiber within me and so I fought and resisted every explanation. Finally she had my parents take me out of the class.

As you can see, religious teaching, as far back as my memory goes has always seemed inconsistent with what my understanding of the "truth" was, and to this day I am still questioning the inconsistency of religion.

Yet even with this mistrust of the teachings, and even with some kind of cognitive sense of the "game" there are brief moments I still find myself wondering. I sometimes find myself getting lost in all the rhetoric. (Therefore I attempt not to "think" too much.)

However, I believe my confusion speaks to the degree of our acculturation, and is a testament of the dedication we will need to overcome it. And we will need to overcome it, if we are to be in our power.

What is most disturbing for me goes beyond the fact that for centuries now "organized religion" has undermined the masses and has attempted to keep us from our true intrinsic power. It has also manipulated man into doing atrocious things to our fellow human beings. There have been more lives lost in the name of religion than by any disease or famine or disaster that has ever occurred on this planet. How else could you get reasonably intelligent men to go and fight wars that are lining the pockets of the elite with riches and misplaced power while destroying their own psyches' as well as the lives of millions while at the same time believing it is for the good of man kind. I ask how can we remain complacent?

I'm not suggesting you give up your "faith", I am simply suggesting that you carefully examine the institution of religion and the misguidance that it seems to foster. Does religion support that you are a Divine Spirit? Does it tell you that within you lives the Spark of the Divine? Does it share with you that you are the light, as every living being that exists **is the light**, or has it encouraged you to believe that your salvation comes from following their light, and the way to salvation is through their teaching? Are you constantly reminded that you are not pure, whole and divine, but rather living a misguided and sinful existence? Yet all along you have been pure, whole and divine. You are pure whole and divine, and have been from the beginning. You just need to remember.

Needless to say religion does not seem to me to be a true path in my evaluation.

What about eastern philosophies?

Those I feel can bring you closer to becoming aware of your true power, but I say this with some reservation as I have only studied the I Ch'ing. I have not studied other eastern philosophies, such as Buddhism or Hinduism nor have I joined any of the groups associated with them. However as I understand it, eastern philosophies consider us to be an aspect of God, where as most western religions or philosophies place God outside of us. For this reason I feel eastern philosophies are closer to my understanding of remembering and activating our "divine" self.

As I stated earlier, I did study the I Ch'ing daily for ten years and I still throw coins now but not on a daily basis. It is through this experience I would consider the I Ch'ing more of a philosophy than a religion, just as I would consider this book more of a philosophy.

When I studied the I Ch'ing daily it was by choice so it never felt like something was being imposed upon me. It seemed like the rudder on my personal voyage which helped to guide me on my spiritual path. It didn't give me any answers, but it supported me in finding answers within myself. It felt like a very old and wise friend that I could talk with everyday. The I Ch'ing advocates meditation, as I believe all eastern philosophies do. It suggests that by becoming still through the practice of meditation you will connect to your center, or your higher self.

This is important because the philosophy suggest you have an ego-self and a higher self, and the ego-self is continually vying for control, and because of this factor the teaching continually guides one towards the path of the higher self. Based on my work with the I Ch'ing and my limited knowledge of Hinduism and Buddhism, I imagine each practiced in their purity can bring you closer to realizing that you are Spirit, as well as assist you in realizing you are a "Spark of the Divine".

I also feel that when the eastern philosophies become highly organized, they are at risk of becoming more like a religion, and risk losing the flow and freedom of the concepts on which they were built. Once an organization gets control of any philosophy, I feel the natural flow is at risk in getting lost to the organization, at which time a fertile bed of dogma can then be birthed.

If we seek our truth in a philosophy that resonates with our inner vibration, a philosophy which utilizes the wisdom of the ancient ones to support us in our re-discovery, I then feel they can be very rewarding to our process.

One of the core teachings of eastern philosophies is their use of meditation. We will discuss meditation later as it can be a useful tool in the re–discovery of our intrinsic power, and our Cosmic Consciousness.

Book Three
Part I

So in conclusion, because of my own experience with the I Ch'ing, I feel the study of eastern philosophies might assist you in opening your doorway to your higher self.

Time to Be ALIVE

Chapter 4

At this moment I feel it is important to again give you a disclaimer regarding this book. I am writing this purely through my perception and it is important for those who read this to understand that these are my perceptions. I know that I have great wisdom. I also am very aware that truth for the most part is very personal. Each person reading this will need to process my thoughts through his or her own filters. When we recognize truth for ourselves it is always felt in a visceral way, and each person needs to recognized those feelings when they happen, for these are your signals and within them your truth. Even though I feel there are many roads to truth, I strongly believe there is One Divine Truth, and our own individual truth will guide us to this.

We are individual "Sparks of the Divine"; we are all one yet we are individuals as well. Our perceptions and thoughts are not necessarily collective, for we see things through our own lens on this planet. My understanding is that eventually we will all come to the same conclusions, but the process whereby we do so, will be different.

Author's Note: *I do recognize I am getting off track again, but when I was talking about the I Ch'ing and I mentioned the ego-self and the higher self. Thoughts started rushing in regarding the ego-self, and how it plays a part in our self discovery. So if the reader would please indulge me as I stray I promise I'll find my way back.*

Here is where ego comes into play. With so much confusion and "bull" to sort through in the process of finding our "true" essence, we may develop an attitude.

This attitude is like an armored shell that helps to prevent the penetration of the restrictions we feel. It is crude, and in many cases can be more harmful than good but probably a necessary way to separate ourselves so we can begin to recognize our power, but we can get lost to it. Often times, we become self-righteous in our concepts, for this in some way gives us a false sense of security for ourselves and it is what I consider the ego. I know, because I certainly possess a healthy one. It takes all the consciousness I have to remember who I am. We are all in the process of remembering who we are intrinsically. Developing an ego, I imagine, has been necessary to that process on this planet. It supports us in our individuality, and probably gives us the courage to stand as one so as to find the whole, but like anything on this planet there has to be balance. The ego, at some point can work to overtake our consciousness if we are not diligent in recognizing when that is happening, and then work at controlling the "ego" self from getting out of hand.

Another issue we have with ego is that more often than not it needs to be right and our ego self will push its will onto others, which often creates more harm than good. When we push our will it often breaks down communication and creates disharmony among people. When we are operating out of our conscious spirit, we can assert our self without the armor of being "right" or self righteous, but instead with an understanding and acceptance of other peoples' points of view.

I find myself being drawn into this all the time, and it still amazes me how often I still push my will with others. How often I still defend my position and close myself off without listening to others. This is the kind of behavior that interferes with relationships, be they with friends, lovers, business associates and on a larger scale other countries. This is the behavior that in my opinion creates wars.

The I Ch'ing encourages discernment, and it has taken me a long time to grasp what it was talking about, but through the writing of this, I understand. Discernment is when I can be in my conscious spirit and understand what is true for me, without getting lost in my ego or the ego of others. I can stand in my power silently and knowingly. Power is not synonymous with being right. Power is the ability to see the larger picture, to have forgiveness and understanding as well as acceptance. Wars are built on greed and ego, so could it be that peace is built on discernment?

I sometimes feel that ego becomes a force within itself, since everything is energy. Suffice to say we also have to deal with "our" ego along with the "other" energy forces that are constantly pressuring us, and keeping us so busy with survival issues that it is difficult to sometimes even take the time to breathe. I also recognize that the ego has many components of the "other" energy forces. Is our "ego center" an aspect of the "other" energy forces living and breathing within us? If we are truly one with the all, and the "all" is the embodiment of "all" things, that would mean that "all" things live within the individual, and we the individual have the components of "all" things living within us.

So in essence we have a component of the "other energy" force vibrationally within us and when we can embrace the elements of the dark and light, good and evil, we bring ourselves to a state of neutrality. In this state of neutrality, we are whole. Once we recognize that we are one, we are able to rise above the petty reality of this dimension and can see it through our higher consciousness, and we are able to discern. I understand this is a lot to absorb, and even harder to describe, yet if we truly believe we are an aspect of the divine it is important to look at all the possibilities because all things come from the source. I realize that this will take several attempts at reading it to even make sense of it but in a sentence or two; if we are truly one with the all then within us exist all energy, and it is incumbent upon us to use our discernment, once we awaken to the consciousness that we are a "spark" of the divine. If we do not practice discernment our energy can easily join forces with the "other" energy forces, participating as well as assisting them with their agenda. Therefore we must remain diligent in utilizing discernment. We must be diligent in making a conscious choice.

Author's Note: *Wow, that was a departure, and we can now get back on track, yet as I am reading what has just been brought through me, I see its' importance and its' relevance to this book. Explore all the possibilities. Listen to all things with your own discernment, your own filters, for your truth will always resonate within you. The key is to listen to yourself, and follow your deeper inner knowing. Listen with your wisdom for you are wise. Again, I remind you that you are a "Spark of the Divine", within you lives your own intrinsic power, your "Cosmic Consciousness". Once you become aware of it, please use it wisely.*

Chapter 5

We left off speaking about eastern philosophies. In that discussion I skimmed over meditation and didn't even touch on chanting, or conscious breathing, so let's look at all these things more closely.

Let us get back to meditation. For centuries the eastern philosophies have used meditation to achieve what they call "nirvana". So what is nirvana? Let's go to the dictionary and get the definition:

Nir va na: the Buddhist idea of heavenly peace; perfect happiness reached by complete absorption of oneself into the supreme universal spirit.

Are we attempting to absorb ourselves into the supreme universal spirit, or to recognize that we are one with the supreme universal spirit? Or are they one in the same?

In the writing of this I realize I use meditation more to relax, and release the stress of my day and return to my center. It is a time when I can receive inspiration to express my own divinity. When I meditate, I can focus on what it is I am attempting to bring into my world. It is a way for me to connect to my "spark" of the divine spirit. It seems like the key phrase here is connect vs. absorb. So would one need to be aware of their divine spark before meditating or would we find it in meditation? What came first the chicken or the egg? These are probably questions best asked within yourself. I certainly know that meditation is a wonderful way to connect with your inner self, but does it facilitate our recognition of spirit? I'm not so certain of that, I think it can, but I also feel it might take a very long time for most individuals to reach that place within themselves through meditation alone, so explore this tool, see for yourself what transpires for you. I am a firm believer in meditation because I feel it can support you in becoming a clearer channel for your own divine wisdom, however there might be more effective ways to accomplish your "quickening."

Chapter 6

How often do you take a walk? How often do you watch a sunrise or sunset? When was the last time you hugged a tree, walk along a beach, star gazed, took a trip to the mountains? When was the last time you experienced nature and the wonder of the planet we live on? Nature is an important component in connecting with your own true *nature*. Nature is a reflection of us when we take the time to experience it. There is a purity and freshness to nature that recurs everyday. If you were to take a walk every morning, you would see that most days the grass is blessed with the dew, and there is a scent of freshness in the air. In nature you see the cycles of life repeat itself yearly, and the phases of the moon repeat themselves every month. The ebb and flow of the tides are connected to the moon. There is a natural balance to nature when left to its own devices. Nature has its moods, and can be quite expressive; for it can be pristine and still, gentle and soothing or chaotic and fierce, it can be healing or angry. It knows how to cleanse itself and the process of continued transformation is reflected in nature. Nature teaches us, reflects us and inspires us. I feel nature is a tool in which our "Spark of the Divine" can be supported and realized.

I cannot end this chapter about nature without discussing vortices. In the beginning of this book when I skimmed over my journeys and the places I have travel, I skimmed and alluded to but did not specifically mention that going to energy spots or vortices on this planet will expand you and open your channels of awareness. Vortices are areas where there is less density as the energy is moving at a faster vibration. Some of the areas where vortices exist have red soil, which means it contains more iron. I have not done any formal research into this, but my intuition tells me that the presence of more iron affects the electro magnetic fields, which in turn affects the density and vibration of those areas. When the body is exposed to a faster vibration, the veils are able to be lifted, or the fog surrounding your inner light becomes lighter and therefore it becomes easier for us to open our channels of awareness. The more open our channels are, the stronger the light, the more aware we become. So perhaps it is time to explore areas around you that are "power points". Mt. Shasta, Sedona, Kona, Machu Picchu, The Yucatan, Stonehenge, The Pyramids, Tibet, are a few of the more talked about areas, but as I've driven through this country and other countries, I've experienced vortices that are powerful, even if they are not spoken of or written about. So I encourage exploring the world and nature for vortices. There is much magic to find as you explore nature and yourself, and I can assure you it will be a most interesting journey.

Book Three
Part I

Book Three
Part I

Chapter 7

Before there were books there were stories and songs. Generation after generation passed their heritage down through the ages with stories and songs. The indigenous cultures around the world would use chanting in their rituals and ceremonies. Eastern philosophies incorporate chanting as part of their meditation process. Along with chanting, ancient cultures were aware of the power of breath. They understood our life force lives within our breath. Could these be gateways to our spiritual essence?

There is a theory that the universe was created with a "bang". Could this be true? There is also much talk about the string theory and if my understanding is correct, the string theory involves vibration as well. Is that the reason the bible begins with the words, "In the beginning there was the "word" and the word was God." Is a word not a sound? Is sound not vibration? Are we not vibration?

Through out this book I have continued to remind you that you are a Spark of the Divine. We are vibration, we are God! So how important is sound to the universe or to us? We are energy, energy is vibration, vibration is sound, and sound is vibration we can hear. Vibration is everything! Sound IS vibration!

How can I best express this? We consist of matter. If you remember in the beginning of the book I gave you the definition of matter, and I am repeating it here.

Matter: "What all (material) things are made of; whatever occupies space and is perceptible to the senses in some way: in modern physics, matter and energy are regarded as equivalents, mutually convertible according to Einstein's formula, E = MC2 (i.e., energy equals mass multiplied by the square of velocity of light); in dualistic thinking, matter is regarded as the opposite of mind, spirit, etc."

I believe this definition brings it all together. We are energy, and energy equals vibration and sound is vibration. We each carry our own "vibrational essence", which is very important in context to this book. Everything on this planet consists of energy. We are directly connected to the "Source" and the "Source" is vibration, as science is proving. We are "one" with the all, and the all is vibration. So you can see how important vibration is and in particular how important your "vibrational essence" is in relationship to the whole. This book is about acknowledging that we are a "Spark" of the Divine, a "Cosmic Consciousness". By understanding that we are energy, I feel it is easier to embrace that we are one with spirit.

We each have our own individual "vibrational essence". This is important as well, because when we consciously activate our vibrational essence it becomes instrumental in living in our "Cosmic Consciousness". When we live in our "vibrational essence" we are living in our "God/Goddess" essence, which means we are living in our power.

I strongly feel that to fully live in our power, we first must acknowledge we are a "Spark" of the Divine, and from that point on, all things are possible. Once we acknowledge this we can use our intention to move forward.

Book Three
Part I

My "vibrational essence" is that of a healer, not a scientist, therefore I cannot elaborate on this further suffice to say intuitively I understand this clearly and science is continuing its research into energy and matter as well as frequencies, vibration and multiple dimensions. Someone once said "Physics is the study that proves what metaphysics already knows." As time goes on, that statement proves to be what I would consider, an accurate assessment.

I recognize that I am not strong in explaining the technical aspects of sound and vibration. As I've admitted earlier, my vibrational essence is that of a healer not a scientist. However it does not take a scientist to understand that we are energy.

I believe the indigenous people around the world also intuitively knew what science is now confirming. To reiterate, we are energy, energy is vibration, and vibration is sound.

For those of you who need more science regarding energy and matter beyond the definitions of the dictionary and Wikipedia, I urge you to search the internet. Search for *quantum physics, The String Theory, Quantum Mechanics, The Big Bang Theory, Michio Kaku, Stephen Hawking, and Einstein.*

Sound is one of the things that allows us to actually feel vibration in our physical body. Sound is an important component to our spiritual well being. Sound can create, sound can destroy and sound can heal. Sound is the great equalizer and can open us to our "harmonic" balance. Since the "Spark of the Divine" is essentially a vibration, is there a natural frequency that governs our individual consciousness? Once we experience that frequency does our power become activated?

I believe the answer is yes. I believe sound, or the perfect vibration or frequency to be the most effective way to open the portals to our inner awareness, and will support you in realizing your own 'vibrational essence".

Author's Note: *While we are talking about vibration, think about what goes on in your daily life. How often do you say I resonate with that? Do we not have a "resonate" understanding of many things in our world? How often have you felt energy in your surroundings? What are you feeling? Can you see it? This in and of itself speaks volumes about the existence of, as well as our conscious awareness of the vibrations that live in our daily lives. Not only do you physically feel vibration through sound, you feel it on an etheric level. Sound, vibration and frequency live within us every moment. We just need to attune ourselves to our deeper inner consciousness, so that we can truly live in our divine "energy."*

So I ask you, can it be that sound, breath and meditation coupled with nature are the keys that unlock the divine within us? There is a magic in three, so is this the alchemical formula that stimulates us to achieve and bring into matter our intentions? Are these the components that will activate our knowing?

Can it be so simple? Do we just need to still ourselves in nature and listen to the harmonics of sound while being conscious of our breath to activate our knowing?

Yes I believe it can be that simple.

Book Three
Part I

Book Three

Part II
Let's Summarize

Chapter 1

We've discussed the need for people to recognize their intrinsic power.

We've talked about "other" energy forces suppressing the power of the masses through manipulation and fear.

We've talked about the need for people on this planet to wake up.

We've talked about concepts that may be used to guide us to our intrinsic power.

We've talk about sound, breath, meditation, nature, energy and vibrations.

There are very different realities being discussed here yet they are intricately intertwined. We talked about the possibility of "outside" forces suppressing our energy and we have talked about different states of awareness. We have discussed how there are those individuals who are still asleep, who have not recognized their power, or even acknowledged that they are a "Spark of the Divine", and there are those who have recognized their intrinsic power to one degree or another, yet don't know how to harness it and utilize it. Wherever we are on the consciousness dial, we need to all Wake Up. Wake Up to the circumstances surrounding us and use our power to change our world into a more conscious and harmonic place to live. We've discussed and we have discussed, but the most important thing we can do now is take action. Time for discussion has come to an end. Find your courage within to vibrate in your essence and "LIVE". This is the true message of this book.

Book Three
Part II

Book Three
Part II

Chapter 2

Since we are summarizing, and since the only basis for my truth is my own process, and this book seems to be born from my reality lets review that as well.

In summery of my own process, I was very young when I recognized my intrinsic power, but I've spent a lifetime learning how to fully accept it and then use it, and I'm still learning. The operative word here is "lifetime". I had to learn to listen to my body and see what resonated as truth for me. Then once I learned how to listen I had to learn to trust. I had to be willing to be different, and when you are young being different seems more like a curse than a badge of honor. When I found I couldn't work a 9 to 5 job I had to delve within my psyche and create another reality for myself, and a career was born. I also had to find the courage to walk a spiritual path for even though I was aware that within me lived the wisdom of the ages, I knew this path might not be the easiest and I had to find my courage, and finding my courage was not a one shot deal, I have to find my courage everyday. And there have been moments, days and even months I was not able to find my courage, so then I needed to call on my internal strength be to bring myself back to my courage, and to this day I am still doing that.

The spiritual path was certainly not the most populated path and because of that, the decision to walk that path took me a few years to decide, yet I did make the choice.

Author's Note: *For those of you who might know me and are familiar with my childhood and my background you can attest to the fact that I've had my own personal struggles and doubts and fears along the way, and this also hindered my decision to walk my spiritual path. So readers, I can tell you from experience, it will not always be easy for you to walk your spiritual path, but I can also assure you that your path will be rich with many wonders and the possibilities that will open for you will be numerous and worth the challenge.*

I feel that if and when more people walk this path, everyone's struggles will disappear, because in some way we would be walking with the flow of the masses instead of against the flow of the masses. So I continue to encourage you to realize your intrinsic innate power, your Cosmic Consciousness, and begin to be ALIVE: Acknowledge & Live In *(your)* Vibrational Essence.

Book Three
Part II

Book Three
Part II

Chapter 3

This book and a lot of information being discussed here is so very relevant to the time in which we presently live. Forty-five years ago the world was a different place, it was moving at a different pace. (Please hear this and pay attention, it was moving at a different pace.) I feel very strongly that time is of the essence now, and that is one of the key reasons I've taken the time to write this book.

Time to Be ALIVE

Book Three

Part III
Awake With Intention
Steps and Guidelines

Chapter 3

PEOPLE NEED TO AWAKEN TO THEIR INTRINSIC POWER, AND IF THEY HAVE ALREADY AWAKENED, THEN THEY NEED TO ACCELERATE THEIR SPIRITUAL AWARENESS AND UTILIZE THE POWER THAT LIVES WITHIN THEM FOR THE HIGHEST GOOD OF ALL.

So how can we do this? We have talked about this, but again, how can we do this? Again, I will turn to my own process.

When I stop and think about my process, I strongly believe that sound and breath were pivotal in my awakening. So then, is sound and breathe pivotal to changing the course we seem to be on? In my most humble of opinions, I believe so. It is clear our present course does not seem to be encouraging us in our power, instead it seems to be taking us farther and farther away from the knowledge and wisdom we came into this planet with. I choose to remind you again that we did come into this planet with our power, even if it was hidden from us, and it is the natural right of every being on this planet to be able to live within their power. So after much thought and discussion with you during this book, these are the steps that I feel will best assist you in finding and utilizing your power.

Time to Be ALIVE

To begin, establish your intention, this is the most important step. We have not talked much about intention, but remember the definition of energy; *"1. force of expression or utterance 2. potential forces; inherent power; capacity for vigorous action 3. strength or power efficiently exerted"*. This is important when we are looking at intention, for intention is the force behind the movement of energy, and we are the energy. Intention is what puts the wheels in motion. Intention is what drives or activates our energy. This is how we manifest our thoughts. So, once a thought is born, as you can see intention is the first step in manifesting it. With out intention it is difficult to drive our energy to create our will. So again, because this is important; intention is the force that drives our energy to manifest!

Once your intention is in place we can begin. Now is when we need to breathe. This is our next step. Breathe from your diaphragm, and bring your breath fully into your lungs. Fill your chest and expand it with your breath and deflate it with your exhale. Practice breathing consciously. The breath opens your body to receiving. Every morning take the time to consciously breathe, then during the day, pay attention to your breath. Ask yourself if your breathing is shallow or is it filling your lungs so that the life force "energy" can be carried through your body. Begin each morning with conscious breath. Do this everyday, and you will see it will make a difference.

The next step is to find the sound that will activate your harmonic frequency and listen to that sound daily. Find a chant; and use that chant to support your process. Repeat the chant three times and do this process at least once a day, if not more. I would suggest you do this process several times a day.

Next, go into nature and connect with your "natural" self. I suggest you go for walks, and while walking you can also breathe and chant. If you do this nature will enhance the process of your breathing and chanting.

Clear your mind with meditation, and while meditating, breath and chant; open your "heart" to the magic that lives within.

This is my recommendation based on personal experience.

Twenty years ago I lived by a lake in the middle of Oakland, California. Everyday for over ten years I woke up and did breathing exercises and chanted; "I Am Spirit, Pure, Clear, Beautiful, Strong" in cycles of three. Eventually I put a melody to this chant and plan to someday record it. Then I would walk to the lake, where I was surrounded by nature and as I walked I was very conscious of my breathing and with the sounds of nature; I was walking as well as engaging in what I would call an "active" meditation process. When I returned home from my walk I read the I Ch'ing and at night I listened to a tape called "Tonal Alchemy" by Tom Kenyon. I'm sure after all the things we have discussed you have some imagination about how powerful that time was for me.

Now after writing this book, I am reminded that I have the formula! I was doing this process daily and it was working. I just need to reinstate it in my daily life.

Time to Be ALIVE

I know the prescription that I wrote above seems so very simple, and it is simple. I would like to remind you of a sentence that I wrote earlier in this book. "The truth is simple but that simplicity is woven into a mass of complexity, and once we break away from the complexity we will be left with the simple truth."

I didn't promise an easy truth, but I promised a simple truth. I believe this to be the simple truth. The choice is yours.

Book Four

Part I
More Insights to Consider

Chapter 1

Before I finish this book I feel compelled to share some other thoughts with you. Again, remember my disclaimer, for these are my thoughts that I am sharing with you, so please use your discernment.

There have been many "new age" teachings that touch on how to use the power that is intrinsic within you, one of the most recent being the movie "The Secret". It touches on wisdom as old as the planet, wisdom that lives within you, wisdom we have touched upon in this book. This I feel is one of the reasons this movie was so successful. It resonates with something deep within. It was marketed with a great deal of emphasis on material wealth, a hook that has often been used to get our attention, and in my opinion a hook that is rapidly becoming archaic.

If you have seen this movie or if you are planning on seeing this movie, I hope that you take from it this understanding. As a being, you have the power to create and to manifest by being in your conscious thought. Once you have a thought it can be realized. I beg of you, please remember that intention is an important element in creating, and manifesting goes beyond the materiel world.

The movie's emphasis was so involved with "money" that I have concerns about the effect it may have on people's psyche if they judge their power by their ability to amass material wealth. I hope people do not step backwards in their spiritual process by using wealth as a basis of spiritual evaluation. Will the true "secret" be lost in disappointment if material wealth is not achieved? Power is so much more than how much money you can earn. Money is energy, it has been created on this planet as most things have been, and it is as illusionary as it is real, but the fact remains it is energy.

I have nothing against money. I happen to like money, and I like having money, especially since this planet has been so focused on it, and everything seems to be linked to it. However, having said that, I learned a very long time ago that money did not fill the emptiness within me; it did not sustain my spiritual needs. Money makes our existence on this planet more pleasant, but I feel that the importance of money has been exaggerated. So much propaganda surrounds money and the belief that when you have money you are successful, and if you are successful, power is within your grasp. I just question what kind of power is it?

As necessary as money is to our existence at this moment on the planet it does not define me anymore than it defines you. I have so many riches other than money that I feel blessed. Yes I have gotten trapped in the illusion that money would bring me happiness, and some how if I could amass great sums of money it would measure my success, but I soon found out how hollow that understanding is. Money is a poor anchor to tie yourself to, for it can vanish, and without your sense of spirit, your sense of oneness, your deep and abiding awareness and knowledge that you are a "spark" of the divine, you might find yourself sinking with the changes that are presently upon us.

The core concept of "The Secret" is correct, we do have the power to manifest and direct our own lives.

It is important for us to grasp the true importance of our power beyond material wealth. We have the power to change the world and the downward spiraling direction in which it seems to be heading. We have the power to heal all things, to forgive all things, to accept all things. For we are the light, we are the salvation. Its not some concept outside of you, it is you. This is the power of "The Secret".

Time to Be ALIVE

Book Four

Part II
Reflections and Conclusions

Chapter 1

So back again to how we can "wake" up. Although I might seem redundant here, it is important that I continue to reiterate the message. I believe for change to happen we must look outside the box. Look beyond our conditioning. We need to breathe and with our breath, listen to our bodies; for our bodies and hearts are talking to us. We need to recognize that we are energy, and intention is the force behind our energy. We need to find and activate our own vibrational essence, and I feel that can be done with sound. There are frequencies being brought into the planet at this time that can open the portals to your inner divinity; to your true intrinsic power. I know this for a fact because I happen to be one of the people producing those frequencies, and my work is available to anyone who chooses to seek it and receive it. Transforming and awakening *"sound"* is definitely coming in to support earth and the beings presently living here. It is time for us to listen, not only to the sound, but it is time to "listen" with our hearts. For too long we have been in our heads, and it seems we have gotten stuck there. So please just move your consciousness to your heart. Ask for the perfect resources to guide you, and they will be there ready and willing to support you and your process. All you need to do is pay attention. Find a way to still your mind and commune with nature, for in its simple elegance you will connect to yourself. Last, but not least open yourself to the possibilities and acknowledge your divinity with the pure intention of your heart.

Chapter 2

Although when I was young I had the awareness of who I was, and I was blessed with many experiences to guide me, my biggest break-through awakening came with the sounds of a voice and a crystal bowl. It was subtle but it was profound. I was not only awakened, I was blessed with the realization that I also have the ability to awaken others through the blessing of my sound as I know I've mentioned before. There is something pure and not of this world in the vibrations that come through me and it is time for me to own this. It has taken me a long time to realize the power that I have as a being, and an even longer time to acknowledge it. This book is a definite way for me to acknowledge my power and hopefully in some small way assist you in finding your power.

At this time there are many people who are beginning to awaken to their gifts, and sound is a wonderful way to feed the sprouts of your awareness. Over the years I've worked at many conferences, and I have listened to many speakers and for that matter many words, but I have noticed a trend over the last four years in regards to the power of Sound. The world is finally awakening to the power of Sound, in relationship to time, space, ancient wisdom, and the future well being of the universe. We have also been awakened to the consciousness that everything is energy, and energy is vibration and sound is vibration we can and do experience. Sound is one of the most powerful realities of our existence. Remember, sound can create; sound can destroy; sound can heal; and sound can bring all things into harmony. Utilize the gift of sound in your life. Remember sound, breath, and nature with meditation; these in my opinion are the keys to awakening, but the true awakening comes when you, you personally have the willingness and the intention to recognize **you** are the power; **you** are a "Spark of the Divine".

Yes people are awakening, I'm not seeing it in the masses yet, but there is a great grass roots movement beginning to happen on the planet, and it is growing with each second and by the time this is publish it will have grown even more. So if all of those people who have begun to recognize their power would devote time to working with beings that are still a bit numb and repressed; if we can share our awakening; energetically we can change the world.

The need for intention is a priority and that is why I continue to encourage you to be willing to open yourself to your power. Your willingness or your "intention" is the ingredient that will make your "spirit" rise. When you are opening your channels, open them with conscious thought. Ask that your channels be opened with the highest and best interest in yourself and all other beings. For as the shifting of earth continues, and the changes become more and more evident, how and what we do with our awakening will have great impact on this planet. I feel if we are conscious and diligent we will manifest ourselves in the best interest of the all, and this dear spirits is something I feel is crucial for our times. Remember the ancient secret; intention will manifest our thoughts.

Can you imagine a planet that has awakened, with the clear intent of using the power of our Cosmic Consciousness for the highest good of all and according to the free will of all?

Book Four
Part II

Harmony does exist outside the repression of the "other" energy forces; outside the ego; outside what my friend David Weber and the Richis would say are "our flow" blockages. HARMONY ALREADY EXISTS. It is not a concept beyond our grasp, it is already a living and breathing energy within us, we just need to awaken to our awareness of it.

I hope that after reading this book you pay attention; pay attention to the ways you and your truth are being manipulated and brainwashed to repress your power. Please just start to pay attention. Pay attention to your everyday life. Look around you with open eyes and see what there is there waiting for you to see. When watching TV, pay attention. Just ask yourself; is this just the most perfect way to keep us numb? Is this a perfect way to manipulate and control? Pay attention! Pay attention to how we are taught in schools. Are we generally asked to memorize instead of question? Pay attention! Pay attention to politics and economics, and ask yourself the difficult questions. Ask yourself if you're being told the truth? Are you being treated with respect and fairness? Look around you! Please just look around you and pay attention!

When you pay attention, the repression seems to be almost everywhere, so we have some work to do, "for the times they are a changing".

It will take some work but if we band together, with a collective intention to awaken and take back our power, and be willing to recognize that for **positive** changes to be made we need to use our power for the highest good of all, then we will have a good chance of assisting as well as affecting the changes that are already in process in our world.

So I end with this challenge as well as this opportunity. Are you ready to change the world?

Book Four

Epilogue

Please accept my heartfelt appreciation for taking the time to read this collection of thoughts. I had suspected when I began writing that there would be a wonderful gift awaiting me at the end of my personal revelations. There is, so thank you all, for I now have a vision of what I can do to support the planet.

I will continue to tone and I will continue to speak my truth. I will tone and speak with the intention to be of service to this planet. I will share my sound and my voice with whoever chooses to receive it.

I will lecture wherever I can find an audience to listen and I will begin a live webcast, so that you can choose to join. I don't know how or when or where or how often yet, but I will speak and I will present a live webcast where people can tone with me. I know that I have a "tone" a tone that can open the portals to peoples' inner dimensions. The more voices that join with me will create an even stronger vibrational field to open the portals of self-awareness and self-realization for anyone who chooses them. We will tone for the world, we will tone with intent. We will send out a frequency that can break apart the band of vibration that is being used to repress us and block us, thus opening a pathway for a more unified and harmonic world to be realized.

Sound carried into the ethers with pure intent by a group of beings using their power to help make our world a more enlightened place. This is my vision, and this will be my reality, so I welcome you all to join me in the "toning" fields. Together we can change the world.

Time to Be ALIVE

Continue to check my website:
www.maryelectra.com for more information.

In the meantime, blessings be with you until we meet again.

In Loving Grace,

Mary Electra,

Tonal Alchemist

www.ingramcontent.com/pod-product-compliance
Lightning Source LLC
Chambersburg PA
CBHW021227090426
42740CB00006B/426